Dynamic Research Support for Academic Libraries

Edited by
Starr Hoffman

face
publ

Published by Facet Publishing,
7 Ridgmount Street, London WC1E 7AE
www.facetpublishing.co.uk

Facet Publishing is wholly owned by CILIP: the Chartered Institute
of Library and Information Professionals.

British Library Cataloguing in Publication Data
A catalogue record for this book is available from
the British Library.

ISBN 978-1-78330-049-5

First published 2016

Text printed on FSC accredited material.

Typeset from editor's files by Flagholme Publishing Services in
10/13 pt Palatino Linotype and Franklin Gothic
Printed and made in Great Britain by CPI Group (UK) Ltd,
Croydon, CR0 4YY.

Every purchase of a Facet book helps to fund CILIP's
advocacy, awareness and accreditation programmes
for information professionals.

Contents

Editor and contributors

Editor

Starr Hoffman PhD MLS MA is Head of Planning and Assessment at the University of Nevada, Las Vegas, where she assesses many activities, including the library's support for and impact on research. Previously she supported data-intensive research as the Journalism and Digital Resources Librarian at Columbia University in New York. Her research interests include the impact of academic libraries on students and faculty, the role of libraries in higher education and models of effective academic leadership. When she's not researching, she's taking photographs and travelling the world.

Contributors

Helene N. Andreassen PhD is a Senior Academic Librarian and subject specialist for linguistics, speech therapy and romance languages at the University Library, UiT The Arctic University of Norway. Apart from doing research on students' pronunciation in foreign-language learning, the majority of her time is currently spent on helping students, from BA to PhD, understand and apply the values of academia.

Jackie Carter PhD MS is Director for Engagement with Research Methods Training at University of Manchester, UK. She supports students, researchers and practitioners to undertake data analysis in social research, especially with quantitative data. Her principal interests are in experiential learning and in progressing from theory to practice in data analysis. She has presented and published on statistical literacy and workplace learning.

Heather Coates MLS MS is the Digital Scholarship and Data Management Librarian at the IUPUI (Indiana University Purdue University Indianapolis)

University Library Center for Digital Scholarship. She provides data services for the campus, advocates for openness in research practices and supports faculty in demonstrating the impact of their research through the responsible use of research metrics.

Fátima Díez-Platas PhD is assistant professor in the Art History Department at the University of Santiago de Compostela (Spain) and principal investigator for the *Biblioteca Digital Ovidiana*, a research project on the illustration of the works of the Roman poet Ovid (www.ovidiuspictus.net). Her research interests lie in ancient Greek iconography, ancient aesthetics, figurate mythology in Classical tradition and the illustration of the works of Ovid. She worked for Perseus Digital Library (Harvard and Yale Universities) and for the *Lexicon Iconographicum Mythologiae Classicae*, and has published books, articles and book chapters on the iconography of Dionysus and the Dionysiac figurative world, on the figure of the Minotaur, and on the illustrated Ovid.

Richard Freeman PhD MLIS MA is the Anthropology Librarian at the University of Florida's George A. Smathers Libraries. He has participated in several library and university-wide groups and workshops pertaining to digital scholarship, an extension of his background in the visual arts and training as a visual anthropologist. He is a photographer/videographer on a National Endowment for the Humanities project to document and analyse Haitian Vodou religious practices in Haiti and Miami, contributing materials to the online Vodou Archive (dloc.com/vodou). He is also on the development team for another NEH grant to complete, promote and teach MassMine, an open-source program allowing academics to mine, analyse and visualize data from Twitter.

Ashley Jester PhD is the Data Services Coordinator in the Digital Social Science Center at Columbia University Libraries/Information Services. In her current role, she directs Quantitative and Qualitative Data Services and supports researchers with finding, using and interpreting data, including consultations on statistical methodology and research design.

Torstein Låg PhD is a Senior Academic Librarian and subject librarian for psychology and psychiatry at the University Library, UiT The Arctic University of Norway. He spends a lot of his time helping students learn and become information-literate and tries to let cognitive and educational psychology inform what he does.

Mariann Løkse MLS MA was recently appointed Head of the Library Services Department at UiT The Arctic University of Norway. She has previously worked as subject librarian for art and literature, and has a strong interest in information literacy teaching. She is the co-author of the book *Information Literacy: how to find, evaluate and cite sources* (2014) and part of the project team behind iKomp.no.

Alberto Santiago Martinez MSIS is the Digital Initiatives Librarian and head of the Digital Scholarship Unit at the Daniel Cosío Villegas Library at El Colegio de México in Mexico City. He has dedicated his efforts towards supporting the use of digital technologies on campus and is one of the founders of RedHD, the Mexican digital humanities network.

Karen Munro MFA MLIS is Head of the University of Oregon Portland Library and Learning Commons, where she provides traditional library and instructional technology support for graduate professional degree programmes. She is interested in better design for public services in academic libraries.

Mark Phillips MLS is the Assistant Dean for Digital Libraries at the University of North Texas (UNT). His current research focuses on digital library infrastructure, web archiving and systems for analysing, identifying and improving metadata related to cultural heritage and digital library collections. He has been involved with the development and operation of the Portal to Texas History, the UNT Digital Library and the Gateway to Oklahoma History, all hosted by the UNT Libraries.

Mark Stenersen BA(Hons) is an information architect and graphic designer and Consultant in Visual Communication at the Centre for Teaching, Learning and Technology, Result, UiT The Arctic University of Norway. His primary function is to help university staff to develop stimulating and engaging online skills with the help of good user experience (UX), interaction (GUI) and visual communication design.

Hannah Tarver MLS is the Department Head of the Digital Projects Unit in the University of North Texas Libraries. She oversees digitization and metadata creation for a variety of materials hosted in the UNT Libraries' Digital Collections. Her professional interests focus on metadata entry and quality assessment, as well as authority control.

Dominic Tate BA is the University of Edinburgh's Scholarly Communications Manager. He provides help and support for staff and students in all matters relating to scholarly communications and research publication, including open access, bibliometrics and copyright. Dominic has previously held similar roles at Royal Holloway, University of London and at the University of Nottingham. Dominic started his career working for open access publisher BioMed Central.

Preface

Rationale for this book

There are many books on reference services, how to support research and learning, and related initiatives such as data services, digital humanities support and data management. However, there are few, if any, that provide illustrative examples of these varied services in one volume, viewing them as correlated, emerging models of research support.

Higher education and academic libraries are in a period of rapid evolution. Technology, pedagogical shifts and programmatic changes in education mean that libraries must continually evaluate and adjust their services to meet new needs. Research and learning across institutions is becoming more team-based, crossing disciplines and dependent on increasingly sophisticated and varied data. To provide valuable services in this shifting, diverse environment, libraries must think about new ways to support research on their campuses, including collaborating across library and departmental boundaries.

This book is intended to enrich and expand your vision of research support in academic libraries by:

- inspiring you to think creatively about new services
- sparking ideas of potential collaborations within and outside the library, increasing awareness of functional areas that are potential key partners
- providing specific examples of new services, as well as the decision-making and implementation process
- providing a broad array of examples across different kinds of institutions
- shifting from a mindset of research and instruction services, metadata creation, data services, etc., as separate initiatives, toward a broad view of 'research support.'

This volume is not intended as a checklist of 'must-haves' for every academic library. Each institution, and each library, serves a different group of students, faculty, and staff, and varies by mission, size, academic focus and more. Thus, there is no 'one size fits all' service model. Instead, these projects and support models are presented to inspire initiatives that fit your specific institution's needs and mission.

'Research support' as defined in this book

As implied above, the phrase 'research support' in this book encompasses more than the traditional academic library definition of 'reference' or 'research and instructional services.'

'Research support' isn't something limited to large research libraries. Academic libraries of all sizes, missions and locations – including liberal arts institutions, community colleges and others that are teaching-focused – are shifting to broader forms of research support. After all, 'research' is merely the pursuit or creation of new knowledge. This quote from Zora Neale Hurston (1942) speaks to a simple passion for this activity, 'Research is formalized curiosity. It is poking and prying with a purpose.' This curiosity takes place on every campus, regardless of its mission or size.

Nor is 'research support' exclusive to the sciences, social sciences, or other disciplines that use quantitative data. The term 'research' is used in this book to describe a wide variety of scholarship across the disciplines. The term 'data' in the following chapters includes not only quantitative data, but also qualitative data, images, literary texts, or anything else that may be an object of study.

Audience

The intended audience for this book includes academic librarians, other LIS professionals, and library or higher education administrators. The book is also relevant as a text for instructors and students in library and information science programs. It will introduce them to the increasingly collaborative and fluid nature of research services in academic libraries, and provide specific case studies that may be discussed in class. As described above, the book is apropriate for a variety of institutions, regardless of location, size or mission.

A global context

Academic libraries do not operate in a geographic vacuum. In this global environment, our students and faculty come from many different countries. Based on their varied backgrounds, our users have different expectations and assumptions about library practices. Therefore, this book was designed with an international audience in mind. Its authors come from several different countries, in an effort to represent a variety of experiences across different institutions and locations.

Overview of contents

This book is divided into three parts. Each part begins with an introduction laying out the theme or theory of that section, paving the way for the chapters that follow. The individual chapters illustrate specific examples of new models of research support. Each chapter describes the model in question, and includes practical information such as decision-making processes, development and implementation.

The introduction, 'A vision for supporting research,' discusses how an exploratory, collaborative library culture contributes to the development of dynamic research services.

Part 1 is titled 'Training and Infrastructure,' and in the introduction I describe the role of staff development and library spaces in research support. Chapter 1, 'Constructing a model for Mexican libraries in the 21st century' by Alberto Santiago Martinez, describes a library renovation and expansion project designed to better support digital scholarship at El Colegio de México (Mexico). Chapter 2, 'Researching illustrated books in art history: a brief history of the Biblioteca Digital Ovidiana project' by Fátima Díez-Platas at the University of Santiago de Compostela (Spain), describes how digitizing a collection of illustrated books has enhanced art history scholarship across Europe. Chapter 3, 'The "Developing Librarian" digital scholarship pilot training project' by Richard Freeman, describes how librarians at the University of Florida (USA) learned digital scholarship skills in order to support their institution's growing research in the digital humanities.

Part 2, titled 'Data services and data literacy,' opens with an introduction by Jackie Carter, University of Manchester on the importance of data support in academic research. Chapter 4, 'Training researchers to manage data for better results, re-use and long-term access' by Heather Coates, provides an example of a data literacy program developed at Indiana University-Purdue University Indianapolis (USA). Chapter 5, 'Data services for the research lifecycle: the Digital Social Science Center' by Ashley Jester, describes a combined research and data services model implemented at Columbia University in the city of New York (USA). In Chapter 6, 'Mapping unusual research needs: supporting GIS across non-traditional disciplines,' Karen Munro details support for architecture and journalism students using geographic information systems (GIS) at the University of Oregon (USA).

In the introduction to Part 3, titled 'Research as a conversation,' I discuss academic library initiatives to support the dissemination, discovery and critical analysis of research. Chapter 7, 'Implementing open access across a large university: a case study,' by Dominic Tate, describes implementing open access for research outputs at the University of Edinburgh (UK). Chapter 8, 'Bridging the gap: easing the transition to higher education with an information literacy MOOC,' by Mariann Løkse, Helene N. Andreassen, Torstein Låg and Mark Stenersen of UiT, The Arctic University of Norway (Norway), describes the development of an online information literacy course. Chapter 9, 'Metadata enhancement through name authority in the UNT Digital Library' by Hannah Tarver and Mark Phillips, describes the importance of descriptive, rich metadata to making research findable at the University of North Texas (USA).

How to use this book

It is our hope that the selective examples provided in this book inspire you to develop new services, to think creatively about your interactions with faculty and students and to reach across library and institutional boundaries to form dynamic collaborations. Think of the following chapters not as strict guidelines, but as jumping-off points from which to build rich services that serve your specific institution best.

Starr Hoffman

Reference

Hurston, Z. N. (1942) *Dust Tracks on a Road: an autobiography*, Harper Perennial.

Introduction: a vision for supporting research

Starr Hoffman

What is 'research support?'

The traditional model of a public services librarian sitting at a desk, answering student questions, no longer adequately captures the experience of many academic librarians. Some still sit at reference desks, but those desks have changed, often incorporating a variety of services such as circulation and technological support. Librarians themselves may be on call nearby while students or paraprofessionals sit at the desk, answering directional and transactional questions. Librarians may find that reference questions swiftly transform into impromptu sessions on information literacy, or tutorials on interpreting quantitative statistics, or methods of sharing research.

In addition to these reference-desk-adjacent inquiries, librarian support for student and faculty work is expanding to include areas such as the digital humanities and data management, which have traditionally been performed by specialists in areas outside the reference and instruction realm. Academic libraries are realizing the power of existing liaison or subject librarian relationships with faculty, and many are mining those relationships to offer discipline-specific support for open access publishing, data use and management, and other services.

Research support isn't something limited to large-scale research libraries. Academic libraries of all sizes, missions and locations – including small liberal arts and community colleges – are shifting to broader forms of research support. After all, 'research' is not something specific to one discipline; it is the pursuit or creation of new knowledge. This idea can also be expressed as 'inquiry,' research as an exploration and process of asking questions (Pagowsky, 2014). Guided inquiry is a learning technique in which students are taught to ask themselves questions such as: 'What do I want to learn?', 'How do I learn it?', 'What did I learn?' and 'How will I use what I learned?' (Kuhlthau, Maniotes and Caspari, 2007).

Likewise, Kenneth Burke's (1974) metaphor of 'research as a conversation' is one that can be applied equally to all disciplines. Burke (1974) describes the research process as being like walking into a room where a conversation has been going on for a while. After listening to the conversation for a while, you join in with your own point of view. Some people agree with you and provide further evidence, while others counter your argument. Nicole Pagowsky (2014) describes this process as 'examining the connections and ongoing narratives between different scholarly pieces'. Instead of merely being consumers of information, this model encourages students to become active critics, engaging with existing scholarly work and in turn themselves creating new knowledge to contribute to the conversation.

Inquiry and research as a conversation are tied intimately to the 'critlib' movement in information literacy, engaging students in critical thinking and questioning traditional notions of authority (Accardi, Drabinski and Kumbier, 2010). Using these 'critlib' methods in information literacy can expand the research conversation to become more diverse and inclusive, as well as challenge students to not merely memorize the indicators of a peer-reviewed scholarly journal, but to create their own criteria for evaluating meaningful and robust scholarship.

As we expand our traditional print-focused mode of information literacy to include media literacy or transliteracy, we must also consider related concepts such as data literacy. Students are faced with an increasing amount and variety of information and upon graduation will be expected to navigate it all with fluency. We must expand our instruction to prepare students to explore and evaluate any kind of information. Thus, through critlib and teaching new forms of literacy, information literacy is also an important part of research support.

Research in our institutions is becoming increasingly team-driven and interdisciplinary. Thus, our users have increasingly sophisticated needs for methodological and analytical support, data management, and research dissemination. Our role as academic librarians is to partner with our students and faculty during this process and provide a holistic suite of research and instructional services. In this context, 'research support' can refer to anything that a library does that supports the activity of scholarship and research at its parent institution. As we develop these services, we should create a library culture that encompasses three themes: exploration, learning and collaboration.

An exploratory culture

Just as research is an iterative process, so should be our exploration and improvement of services. Instead of being static, we should evolve with our institution and respond to our users' needs by continuously improving our services.

We can accomplish this iterative change through several methods. First, we must encourage a culture of exploration. As librarians, it's important that we feel free to play, to experiment with new technologies and new ideas. In order for our constituents to see research libraries as dynamic spaces where research happens, we must cultivate our own interests and explore new things.

It is important to create an environment where risk is seen as positive. In this environment, a new library service that draws only a few users or has an otherwise disappointing outcome should not be labelled a failure. Rather, such an outcome should be viewed as a data point from which we learn, adjust and try something new. That's what research is, trying something with an uncertain outcome – whether the results are positive or negative, they deserve to be discussed and utilized. Nothing can be learned without making some mistakes.

This idea of exploration segues into the concept of responsiveness. Higher education is in a period of immense change. As libraries, we're constantly affected by new technologies and evolving methods of information dissemination. We must be observant of these changing student and faculty needs, and be ready to respond quickly. Just as we use feedback in reference interviews to respond and adapt on the fly to patron needs, we should draw on that skill to adapt our services as needed.

This continual exploratory process of response and risk must be tied to assessment. Assessment is also iterative; as we observe our constituents' changing needs and respond with new services, we continually assess their outcomes by collecting evidence. In turn we use that data to improve the service, thus continually evolving – assessment should not be a circle, but rather a spiral. We assess in order to use that evidence to act upon and create something new the next time around.

Everyone in the library should be a partner in this process. Just because the term 'assessment' is assigned to a specific position or department doesn't mean that this activity is relegated to only that person or that area. Assessment is a process in which we are all collaboratively involved, because it affects how we move forward. Even those who aren't directly involved in assessment planning or the data collection process should be invested in the assessment results, using them to inform what is done and how it is accomplished. Assessment makes our initial exploration relevant and meaningful, and helps us to continuously evolve and move forward.

A culture of learning

This culture of exploration is intimately connected to the concept of lifelong, continual learning. As a library, we should foster a learning culture not only among students and faculty, but also among ourselves as librarians. By encouraging growth in each other, we are poised to reskill ourselves to meet new research needs and thus become more effective partners in our institutions.

Community is an important aspect of fostering a learning culture. As a profession, librarianship is good at the individual level of professional development. However, we should also harness the power of community, viewing our colleagues as learning partners. For many, it is easier to learn in an environment in which others are also learning. A learning community, whether formal or informal, provides encouragement, companionship and guidance. Community members can help each other through difficult concepts or technologies, as well as keep one another accountable for their learning.

There are multiple ways to create learning communities. Groups can be formed within functional library divisions, or across the libraries. These groups may be formed to explore a specific skill or technology, may be broadly exploratory (without a specific skill in mind), or may be designed to produce a specific research output. Such groups are most effective when driven by their members, created out of their own shared desire to learn, rather than dictated by management. The community's learning goal may be influenced by institutional needs, but ultimately will be driven and shaped by its members' interests and passions.

An example of such a group is the 'Developing Librarian' project undertaken by Columbia University Libraries' Humanities and History Team (2013). This group of librarians decided to undertake a digital humanities project in order to reskill themselves to support similar scholarly work. As an added benefit, the digital humanities outcome itself, a digital history of the Morningside Heights neighbourhood that surrounds Columbia's campus, is itself a valuable research output that provides value back to the community. This project has capitalized on existing librarian subject expertise and local collections, while also training librarians in software (like Omeka) and various skills (such as manipulating and cleaning digital assets). This kind of reskilling, particularly for liaison or subject expert librarians, provides nearly unlimited opportunities for libraries to support research (Aukland, 2012; Jaguszewski and Williams, 2013; Schonfeld and Rutner, 2012).

Collaboration and engagement

As the role of liaison librarians evolves, we must collaborate and engage with the university as true partners. If we look for examples, we will find a variety of partnering models. A classic example is formal physical embedding, a librarian who has an assigned location and office hours in an academic department. Such collocation of librarians, students and faculty enables embedded librarians to be effective, visible partners in department activities. It also facilitates librarian familiarity with a discipline's research processes and unique needs. However, informal engagement can be just as significant. This might be regularly engaging with faculty and students in their academic space, for instance, by attending events and meetings. It's possible to be a part of that academic culture without the structure of set hours or location. An alternative model of informal embedding might be setting up office hours in the public area of an academic department, similar to the office hours that faculty provide for their students. The end goal of these activities is to make the library's research support more visible, and to find new opportunities in which to engage as research partners.

Alternatively, engagement can be expanded to partner with support departments like centres for instruction, academic support centres and student affairs offices. Libraries share common goals with many of these areas, particularly in supporting student learning and faculty research; partnering on events and services could be powerful. In particular, co-hosting workshops and other events could increase the reach of both the library and the participating department, while incurring only half the cost and/or staff involvement that each department would typically sustain. Libraries could work with these support departments to potentially develop new, collaborative services that are highly flexible.

Such collaborations might extend to offices for sponsored research, partnering to share information and services on locating grants, writing proposals, and data management. In institutions where institutional repositories or data management are handled by external, non-library departments, libraries could consider partnering with them to create seamless research support structures for faculty. Even the simple act of sharing information with external departments – telling them about library services and asking about what they offer – can increase referrals and help both the library and external departments reach a broader audience.

True collaboration lies in librarians paralleling faculty as researchers. The future of the reference librarian lies in becoming an integral partner in the research process of students and faculty. Librarians are highly skilled in organizing, synthesizing and disseminating information, all of which are key research skills. Many academic librarians have additional expertise in subject areas, making them ideal research partners. This partnership might take formal shape as a librarian becoming co-investigator on a grant-funded research project, or may be as simple as a series of conversations about methodology.

This idea of research partners builds on the recent evolution of the liaison or subject librarian as a partner with other library functional areas, such as data management and scholarly communication. Liaison librarians must partner with library specialists in these areas to provide dynamic, comprehensive research services. Liaisons may partner with specialists by helping draft data management plans, consulting on copyright and helping disseminate research in institutional repositories and open access journals. As cited earlier, recent reports on liaison librarian roles from the Association of Research Libraries (Jaguszewski and Williams, 2013) and Research Libraries UK (Aukland, 2012) document examples of collaborative reskilling of subject specialists in these areas, thus broadening the types of academic library research support.

To further emphasize the central role of the library in the research process, many institutions are sharing research outputs in library space, by hosting researcher lectures and sharing research images or posters in library spaces. Other approaches could include sharing research results from a variety of disciplines in an interdisciplinary lightning round or pecha kucha session (brief presentations of 20 slides shown for 20 seconds each).

Librarians can also partner with faculty on instruction. Many institutions have already begun this by embedding information literacy into their undergraduate curriculum. As librarians form deeper relationships with faculty, they can seek additional opportunities to engage with their courses. Research methods courses are natural places to insert information literacy, to either engage with a class several times or to co-teach it with a faculty member. Incorporating the library into these foundational research courses ensures that students understand not only where to find information, but more importantly how to evaluate and process it. Additionally, as subject experts, librarians may seek opportunities to guest-lecture for courses, to share and expand on their specific subject expertise.

These are merely some of the broad spectrum of ways in which libraries can engage and collaborate as research partners with students and faculty, and across the institution.

Do less, but deeper

For far too long, the mantra in many libraries has been 'do more with less,' the idea that we should somehow solve shrinking budgets by creating more projects and services despite time and budget constraints. This inevitably results in a slew of half-finished projects and frazzled librarians. While the desire to do more is creditable and speaks to passion for librarianship, all too often implementing 'more with less' results in a lack of buy-in, creates a perception that administration doesn't understand the realities of staff workloads and ultimately can lead to staff burnout. Our librarians and staff deserve more respect and care than this model allows.

Aside from considerations of limited time, staff, and money, there is good reason to limit what is accomplished in libraries. Each academic library resides in a specific situation with a unique collection, has specific strengths, and serves a parent institution of a certain size, funding control, student body and mission. Institutions are best served by focus – by limiting library services to what institutions need most and what libraries do best. 'What institutions need most' means focusing on the parent institution's programmatic priorities and strengths as well as its users' most frequent needs. 'What libraries do best' means assessing staff talents, collection strengths and the realistic possibilities of physical spaces to provide services in which librarians and library spaces shine. We shouldn't try to recreate what every other library is doing – instead, we should look for what our specific institution needs, and what we already do best, and tailor our approach accordingly. Relevant self-assessment questions include:

- What is the one thing that is most important for our library users?
- What activity takes up the most time in our library – is it related to that most important user need?
- If not, how can we reduce the time spent on this activity?

By limiting the services provided and the projects created, libraries can enable their staff to spend more time and care on each. This results in services that are well thought-out and planned, regularly assessed and fluidly responsive to changing user needs. Further, it enables staff to maintain passion and enthusiasm for the work they do, ensuring that they are able to do it at a higher quality than if their attention and energy are split between a myriad activities. Prioritization and restraint are valuable tools for academic libraries. Libraries can prioritize by asking questions such as:

- Does this service support the mission and vision of the library? Of our parent institution?
- Is it meaningful?
- What may we have to cut or reduce to accomplish this?
- How can we best utilize our existing resources, staff expertise and talents, collection strengths, facility advantages?
- What is the measurable gain for our constituents?

The ideas presented in the following chapters are presented as case studies, examples from which each may pull what is most relevant for their situation.

They are not intended as a list of required activities, but as a menu from which to select what fits best. Adapt these ideas as needed, and apply the 'small apartment' mantra – for every new thing, one old thing must go. This idea is as relevant for library initiatives as it is for shoes!

Conclusion

Our role as academic librarians is to explore, to learn, to collaborate as true partners in the university. There is no single magical answer or essential service, nor can any academic library implement all of the ideas in this volume. Each institution, and each library, serves a different constituency. Our institutions vary by mission, size, funding control, academic focus, curricular strength, student body, region and more. There is no 'one size fits all' for academic libraries: they are as varied as the parent institutions that they serve. By investigating academic library trends and casting them in the environment of our institutions, we can determine which services work best in our specific context.

We must be ready to learn, evolve, and to change as our institution changes. As librarians, we are uniquely suited for this. We are trained to seek out, to learn, and we are passionate about this work. We must channel these talents and create strong relationships in order to support a thriving learning and research culture at our institutions.

References and further reading

Accardi, M. T., Drabinski, E. and Kumbier, A. (2010) *Critical Library Instruction: theories and methods*, Duluth, MN, Library Juice Press.

Aukland, M. (2012) *Re-skilling for Research*, London, UK, Research Libraries UK.

Bakkalbasi, N., Jaggars, D. and Rockenbach, B. (2015) Re-skilling for the Digital Humanities: measuring skills, engagement, and learning, *Library Management*, **36** (3), 208–14, www.emeraldinsight.com/doi/abs/10.1108/LM-09-2014-0109.

Burke, K. (1974) *The Philosophy of Literary Form: studies in symbolic action*, 3rd edn, Berkeley, CA, University of California Press.

Columbia University Libraries' Humanities and History Team (2013) The Developing Librarian Project, *dh+lib: where the digital humanities and librarians meet* (blog), 1 July, Chicago, IL, Association of College and Research Libraries (ACRL), http://acrl.ala.org/dh/2013/07/01/the-developing-librarian-project.

Jaguszewski, J. M. and Williams, K. (2013) *New Roles for New Times: transforming liaison roles in research libraries*, Washington, DC, Association of Research Libraries, www.arl.org/component/content/article/6/2893.

Kuhlthau, C. C., Maniotes, L. K. and Caspari, A. K. (2007) *Guided Inquiry: learning in the 21st century*, Westport, CT, Libraries Unlimited.

Pagowksy, N. (2014) #acrlilrevisions next steps, (blog, Nicole Pagowsky), http://
pumpedlibrarian.blogspot.com/2014/12/acrlilrevisions-next-steps.html.

Schonfeld, R. C. and Rutner, J. (2012) *Supporting the Changing Research Practices of
Historians: final report from ITHAKA S+R*, New York, NY, ITHAKA S+R.

PART 1

Training and infrastructure

Introduction to Part 1

Starr Hoffman

Often, articles and books on research support in academic libraries focus on services. While services and service models will certainly be explored in later sections of this book, this initial section takes a closer look at more fundamental concerns: library infrastructure and training librarians for new support models.

Planning for change

Looking at training and infrastructure necessitates first taking a holistic view of our libraries through the lens of organizational development. The key goal that organizational development seeks to achieve is to become an adaptive, flexible organization, to continuously improve. Why is continual improvement needed in academic libraries? It's needed because we operate in a culture of change.

Higher education is in a state of flux, seeking ways to be more transparent, accountable and cost-effective. As new practices in teaching, learning and research continually emerge, student and faculty work is being shaped by them. As libraries, we're constantly affected by new technologies and evolving methods of information dissemination. Library budgets are likely to never return to their pre-recession highs. We must be observant of these conditions, and of changing student and faculty needs, and be ready to respond quickly.

Planning for change should begin by evaluating the library's current infrastructure, staff skills and institutional needs. Evaluating the infrastructure might include listing any necessary maintenance activities, as well as assessing how the current space is used. Space assessments could include ethnographic observations of student and faculty use of library space, such as those detailed by Nancy Fried Foster and Susan Gibbons in their ground-breaking study at the University of Rochester (Foster and Gibbons, 2007).

Following the work of Foster and Gibbons, ethnographic and observation studies are increasing in popularity (Council on Library and Information Resources, 2012). These methods involve observing users in the library space (and in some cases, how they research and learn outside the library), to learn more about their habits and values. These methods include taking note of where users are in the library space and what they are doing in it at different times throughout the day. They also include wayfinding studies, observing how users move through space in the library. Some projects use GPS units to observe student movement and study habits throughout the campus, to ascertain hidden needs that the library doesn't currently meet (Kinsley et al., 2014). Foster's methods also encourage users' input in space design, using techniques such as charrettes (collaborative design meetings) and student space proposals. These should be considered alongside evidence of faculty and student needs as exhibited in instruments such as the 'Library as Place' dimension in LibQUAL+, as well as institution-wide reports and discussions (Association of Research Libraries, n.d.).

Evaluating librarian skills can be done through a skills inventory. Broadly defined skills assessment tools already exist, but for this purpose creating one tailored to the specific situation may be more useful. Skills inventories may include 'soft skills' like leadership and communication as well as experience with specific software, devices, research methodologies, content areas, etc. Having a list of software, devices and skills perceived to be potentially useful for future services can be helpful. However, it is also useful to include blank space where librarians can include additional skills, particularly ones that might fill unanticipated needs (for instance, a librarian with graphic design experience could create promotional fliers for new research services). Including a scale, such as 'novice, intermediate, or advanced,' can encourage librarians to include skills of which they may not yet be confident, but with which they nonetheless have familiarity. Such inventories can reveal previously hidden skills and talents that may be tapped.

Evaluating the institution's needs should be performed on a variety of levels. A clear place to begin, as mentioned earlier, is by reading institutional reports, including strategic plans and departmental self-studies. Any available documentation related to accreditation or curriculum reviews may be helpful. Faculty needs are often expressed in bodies such as the Faculty Senate. Student needs may be revealed by careful reading of the student newspaper, as well as the minutes of meetings of student government associations and other student organizations. Additionally, individual interviews and focus groups with students and faculty may be used to gain further insight into recurring themes.

As with any decision, all of this information will be used to inform what to prioritize, what to delay and what to give up. The skills inventory may identify multiple opportunities to capitalize on existing staff competencies, but these must be balanced against the greatest needs of the institution.

Considering the infrastructure

Usually, the older our institutions become, the more building maintenance issues we must face. All too often, when budgets are low, regular maintenance and repairs are deferred indefinitely, causing even worse issues decades later (Brown and Gamber, 2002). Additionally, many libraries were designed for the era of the printed book, with lots of shelving, few areas for group interaction, and few windows, which doesn't lend them well to modern library activities. However, even libraries built just a few years ago may face issues of infrastructure, as technological advances and use patterns change ever more rapidly. Building accessibility is an additional concern, beyond considerations of how the space fits the current research needs of students and faculty. Clients with special needs must be considered in all areas and for all services and collections, not only when considering entryways and elevators (Henning, 2015).

An organization-wide focus on user experience is an emerging library trend related to infrastructure (Schmidt, 2011; Schmidt and Etches, 2012; Walton, 2015). In studies of academic libraries, a common finding is that there is no single best user experience. For instance, the same user survey may indicate strong student preference for group space and simultaneous strong student preference for individual space. Academic libraries serve multiple user groups, and even within those groups, users often have very different feelings and desires about their library experience. Thus, situational design is an important goal – that is, designing services, spaces and collections in such a way that users can create the experience that they want.

A popular interpretation of this principle is designing library spaces to be flexible, with modular or moveable furniture and fixtures, such as mobile whiteboards or dividers (Bazillion, 2001). (This is a physical parallel to responsive web design, which automatically adjusts the library website to the screen size of the user's computer or mobile device.) Ideally, these moveable pieces are placed in large, open spaces which can then be easily reconfigured for a variety of uses. The first goal of this situational design is to allow for users to create the space and experience that they want. But a second benefit is that open spaces and non-permanent fixtures mean that the space will potentially allow for future growth, for ways of using libraries that we cannot yet imagine (Henning, 2015). There is no way to effectively 'future-proof' a library building, of course, but creating flexible spaces is a step toward that goal.

Training for new research models

As mentioned in the introduction to this volume, recent reports have popularized the idea of reskilling liaison or subject expert librarians (Aukland, 2012; Daniel et al., 2011; Jaguszewski and Williams, 2013). Often, this entails utilizing their subject expertise in new ways, such as curating online exhibits, creating digital collections, or supporting faculty in digital humanities scholarship. These reports emphasize that because the advent of online searching and more sophisticated library catalogues are beginning to shift the emphasis of reference transactions away from discovery, librarians should be trained in new support activities. The key in this is both to find effective reskilling methods and to repurpose existing subject expertise and skills as much as possible.

There are a variety of options available for training. In the case of learning new tools or software, these can be accomplished through hands-on workshops, webinars, handouts, tutorials or information discussions (Bresnahan and Johnson, 2013). One chapter in this section will speak specifically about the efficacy of a reskilling through a learning community that worked on a project, and incorporated a variety of these training methods throughout the process.

The pivotal role that library administration plays in learning communities like these is providing support. This support includes providing adequate staff time and space for this exploration (Bakkalbasi, Jaggars and Rockenbach, 2015; Columbia University Libraries' Humanities and History Team, 2013). Support may additionally include financial or other resource support and recognizing staff for their accomplishments in these groups. However, the creation and direction of these groups should be initiated by group members, so that the learning goals are created by library faculty and staff, not by managers or administrators. Learning is most effective when it is self-directed.

Fostering learning communities is just one method of support reskilling and development. Other methods include providing time and funding for conferences and formal training opportunities. Even more important is indicating the value that library administration places on developing and reskilling their staff. This value can be indicated and spread throughout the organization by recognizing staff participation in research and learning activities and encouraging staff to share their learning experiences with the rest of the library (Oyelude, 2015).

Recognizing staff research and sharing learning experiences can be encouraged through regularly disseminating staff presentations and publications, as well as publicizing staff involvement in professional organizations. Internal poster presentations and post-conference debriefing sessions allow staff to share their research with each other, and to spread positive learning outcomes from conferences and training throughout the library.

Ultimately, developing an engaged and skilled library staff is the key to creating a thriving library culture that provides dynamic research support.

References

Association of Research Libraries (n.d.) Survey FAQs, *LibQUAL+*, www.libqual.org/about/about_survey/faq_survey.

Auckland, M. (2012) *Re-skilling for Research*, London, UK, Research Libraries UK.

Bakkalbasi, N., Jaggars, D. and Rockenbach, B. (2015) Re-skilling for the Digital Humanities: measuring skills, engagement, and learning, *Library Management*, **36** (3), 208–14, www.emeraldinsight.com/doi/abs/10.1108/LM-09-2014-0109.

Bazillion, R. J. (2001) Academic Libraries in the Digital Revolution: libraries in the midst of revolution need new ways of thinking about their mission, *Educause Quarterly*, **1**, 51–5, http://net.educause.edu/ir/library/pdf/eqm0119.pdf.

Bresnahan, M. M. and Johnson, A. M. (2013) Assessing Scholarly Communication and Research Data Training Needs, *Reference Services Review*, **41** (3), 413–33, DOI 10.1108/RSR-01-2013-0003.

Brown, W. A. and Gamber, C. (2002) *Cost Containment in Higher Education: issues and recommendations*, San Francisco, CA, Jossey-Bass.

Columbia University Libraries' Humanities and History Team (2013) The Developing Librarian Project, *dh+lib: where the digital humanities and librarians meet* (blog), 1 July, Chicago, IL, Association of College and Research Libraries (ACRL), http://acrl.ala.org/dh/2013/07/01/the-developing-librarian-project.

Council on Library and Information Resources (2012) *Participatory Design in Academic Libraries: methods, findings, and implementations*, www.clir.org/pubs/reports/pub155.

Daniel, L., Ferguson, J., Gray, T., Harvey, A., Harvey, D., Pachtner, D. and Troost, K. (2011) *Engaging with Library Users: sharpening our vision as subject librarians for the Duke University Libraries*, Durham, NC, Duke University Libraries: Collections and User Services Council.

Foster, N. F. and Gibbons, S., eds (2007) *Studying Students: the undergraduate research project at the University of Rochester*, Chicago, IL, Association of College and Research Libraries, www.ala.org/acrl/sites/ala.org.acrl/files/content/publications/booksanddigitalresources/digital/Foster-Gibbons_cmpd.pdf.

Henning, J. (2015) Future Library Space: renovations to meet client needs, paper presented 16 August at the IFLA World Library and Information Conference 2015, *Dynamic Libraries: Access, Development and Transformation*, Cape Town, South Africa, http://library.ifla.org/1142/1/075-henning-en.pdf.

Jaguszewski, J. M. and Williams, K. (2013) *New Roles for New Times: transforming liaison roles in research libraries*, Washington, DC, Association of Research Libraries, www.arl.org/component/content/article/6/2893.

Kinsley, K. M., Besara, R., Scheel, A., Colvin, G., Evans Brady, J. and Burel, M. (2014)

Graduate Conversations: assessing the space needs of graduate students, *Library Faculty Publications*, Paper 15,
http://diginole.lib.fsu.edu/library_faculty_publications/15.

Oyelude, A. (2015) Data Professionals' Training Challenges in Dynamic Work Environments, paper presented 4 June at the IASSIST Conference, *Bridging the Data Divide: data in the international context*, Minneapolis, MN.

Schmidt, A. (2011) Is Your Library Ready for a UX Librarian?: the UX experience, *Library Journal*, **18** (24), http://lj.libraryjournal.com/2011/11/opinion/aaron-schmidt/is-your-library-ready-for-a-ux-librarian.

Schmidt, A. and Etches, A. (2012) *User Experience (UX) Design for Libraries*, London, UK, Facet Publishing.

Walton, G. (2015) What User Experience (UX) Means for Academic Libraries, *New Review of Academic Librarianship*, **21**, 1–3.

CHAPTER 1

Constructing a model for Mexican libraries in the 21st century

Alberto Santiago Martinez

Introduction

Changes in the academic practices of universities are requiring the research libraries that support them to transform in order to provide effective and relevant information services. The rise of digital scholarship in social sciences and humanities requires liberal arts institutions to adopt new strategies for conducting research and instruction. Unfortunately, older libraries are often ill-equipped to support the ever-growing needs of their academic communities. This is especially true in countries such as Mexico, where many research libraries continue to uphold traditional service models. This can pose a significant challenge to the knowledge production and dissemination of the local campus community.

This chapter presents a case study of the library renovation and expansion project implemented at The Daniel Cosío Villegas Library at El Colegio de México (Colmex) in Mexico City. In 2012, the university took on the task of renovating and expanding its sole library. The project goal was to create a flagship library that would be a model for 21st-century research libraries across Mexico. However, defining what a Mexican library should be for the 21st century is a daunting task, given that national literature on the topic is sparse and international models may not be relevant for Mexican libraries in general, nor in the unique situation of the Colmex library. The library conducted a series of studies to understand the behaviour, opinions and requirements of the campus community with the intention of creating a user-oriented solution.

Through an iterative planning process, we developed a plan that pairs traditional library services (to which the community was accustomed) along with new types of digital scholarship support services. This was accomplished in part by designing spaces that adapt to evolving research and pedagogical practices while also considering the library's regional context. The result is a plan that will transform the traditional model of the Daniel Cosío Villegas Library into one that caters to new modes of information access, interaction, learning, creation and dissemination. Implementing this plan will result in significant organizational restructuring as well as the acquisition and the development of new technologies, tools and services.

Background

Colmex is a prestigious institute of higher learning in Mexico City that is dedicated to research and instruction in the humanities and social sciences. The academic community is composed of approximately 443 students, of which 205 are pursuing PhDs, 164 pursuing master's, and 64 earning bachelor's degrees. The teaching and research faculty is composed of 399 professors. Campus community members come from North and South America, Africa and Europe. However, they are principally of Mexican and Latin American descent.

Courses are offered in political science, demography, economics, Asian and African studies, history, linguistics, literature and sociology. Undergraduate courses are offered in public administration and international studies. Scholarly communication on campus is usually carried out through traditional avenues including print publications, academic gatherings, round-table discussions and seminars.

The university's only building was designed by the architects Abraham Zabludovsky and Teodoro González de León and was constructed in 1976. The building is a registered landmark and was featured in a 2015 architectural exhibition at the Museum of Modern Art in New York (Cruz, 2015). The original design requirements specified that the architecture should not only support traditional university activities, but also be built to foster interdisciplinary interaction between the entire campus community (Cruz, 2014).

The Daniel Cosío Villegas Library is the university's sole library building. Since its foundation in 1976, university administrators have recognized the importance of the library's role in supporting academic activities on campus. As such, the library is centrally located and comprises 30% of the building's structure. The library's personnel includes 18 academic librarians with faculty standing, three IT professionals, and 80 clerical staff and paraprofessionals. The library's curatorial efforts have transformed its collection into one of the most important Latin American collections in its areas of specialism. The library has played an important role for both the campus and national academic library practices by driving various national initiatives such as the 1990s migration to OPACs (online publicly accessible catalogues), which spurred other institutions to follow.

The expansion project

The original library's materials storage capacity measured 27,000 linear metres (nearly 88,600 linear feet), with a maximum capacity of close to 700,000 volumes. The library was designed with an expected collection growth capacity of 20 years. However, this capacity was not reached until 2003. When it reached its limit Aria Garza Mercado, the original library planner, took on the task of designing a new library expansion plan to support growth until 2024. Unfortunately, this plan was never implemented, given the lack of resources and budget. In 2012, the university president successfully secured financing for library expansion from the federal government and the university office of development. Following this, the library director was charged with the task of creating the renovation and expansion plan.

A committee composed of library faculty was created to assist the library director in creating the plan, with the aim of outlining the library's needs. The specific objective and scope of the committee were as follows:

- define spaces for the new library expansion
- propose equipment and furniture
- propose spaces.

The director faced the challenge of creating a plan as soon as possible; due to political and legal constraints, the renovation had to be completed within three years. Passing this deadline could result in the loss of money and failure to complete the project.

Given infrastructure needs and additional funding from the university IT unit and the office of development, the project's scope expanded to include a renovation of the library's public space and the entire electrical and communications infrastructure. Due to the project's extent and its impact on the campus, the committee decided to integrate the governing body, architects, university IT, and building and maintenance personnel into the committee to assist in the project definition. The definition of the project was specified by the core committee members with the aid of the non-library stakeholders.

Process

Although there was no formalized project management plan, due to the ever-changing dynamic and relatively short time to develop and implement the renovation, the committee members adopted an agile, iterative process that for the purposes of this chapter will be designated as 'Rounds'. Since our scope was limited to creating documentation, we did not contemplate a review of the implementation. However, the proposed architectural solutions were submitted for review to the library committee before being approved by the university governing body.

Round 1

The committee began with a series of informal brainstorming sessions in which the entire library staff was encouraged to propose ideas regardless of price, space or viability. The intent of the exercise was to gauge perceptions of what the library should be and for committee members with differing views to come to an understanding. Many of the proposed ideas were based on literature reviews and on visits to other institutions. Ideas included building a space for a café, constructing a research commons and creating a fully fledged multimedia production studio. Additionally, specific library models were also proposed that included the learning resource centre (Martín, 2008) and the commons model (McMullen, 2008).

Simultaneously, the committee conducted a thorough literature review of research library trends. Committee members visited libraries both in Mexico and the USA and attended workshops on academic and research library building projects. Much of the literature reported that both pedagogy and research were increasingly becoming more collaborative, while other reports declared that 'collaboration should undergird all strategic developments of the university, especially at the service function level' (Dillon, 2008; DEFF, 2009). Libraries are increasingly challenged to rethink their role on campus and as an institution (Dillon, 2008). While many library missions are evolving, the library should continue to be the 'locus of expertise and innovation regarding scholarly information, how to find it, and how to use it' (Courant, 2008). The notion of library as a space for books is being challenged, as libraries increasingly acquire new types of resources both physical and digital (Neal, 2012). A new preference for digital materials is converting traditional ideas of the library as a storehouse for information into an institution dedicated to digitizing and opening new forms of interaction and access to resources. There seems to be a pattern in library building projects. For example, Andrew McDonald (2006) specifies key elements that should be considered during the planning process of a library building project. These elements include creating spaces that are functional, adaptable, varied, interactive, efficient, and suitable for information technology, and that have 'oomph.' This was echoed by Steelcase (2013), whose white paper stated that library spaces should be adaptable, furniture should foment collaboration and interaction, and libraries should be generally aesthetically pleasing.

The planning committee conducted a series of informal interviews with various reference librarians, library co-ordinators and the faculty to understand the needs of the community. This exercise revealed a trend among faculty, who were becoming increasingly involved or interested in digital projects. Many tenured faculty members were beginning to request assistance with the creation of personal websites, thematic blogs, publishing e-books, online video interviews and presentations, and the use of computing resources to work with datasets both for research and communication.

Although the university faculty has been working with digital technologies since the 1970s, it wasn't until the mid-2000s that a majority of the tenured faculty began leveraging technologies for academic purposes (Lara, 2015). Such projects include Lingmex (an online linguistic bibliographic database), a digital library focusing on the history of petroleum in Mexico, quantitative economic history databases and primary resource databases for the study of armed political movements in Latin America (de León Portilla, 2012). Similarly, in 2012, the university created a digital education programme dedicated to recording and broadcasting video lectures by notable academic figures both on campus and nationally. The programme has met with much success. In the majority of these cases, the library played a significant role as collaborators, project leaders, programmers and evaluators, and as resource curators.

The library has pioneered digital innovation both nationally and locally. It was the first among its peer institutions to migrate to an OPAC in the 1990s and paved the way for standardized cataloguing processes in Mexico (Arriola Navarrete, 2002). Its first non-OPAC digital project began in 1998 with the digitization and creation of Legislación Mexicana, a digital edition that allowed full-text access and searching of Mexico's legislation from 1687 to 1902. Since then, the library has participated in various digitization projects that include participation in The Biblioteca Cervantes Project and the digitization of the university's complete body of academic journals, dissertations and theses. The library has also participated in and led various digital initiatives nationally to establish Mexican digital libraries, repositories and information access networks.

The digitization of the library resources was done through subcontracting and at an informal digitization unit operated by a two-person team working with a flatbed scanner. The majority of digital projects on campus were carried out in an ad hoc fashion. Decision-making in regard to digitization, metadata creations and systems development was done without documentation or formalized workflows, and with little regard to long-term access, continued growth or systems maintenance and support. Nonetheless, these projects demonstrated the library's capacity to innovate and increased visibility and access for the university's intellectual works and information resources, both to academics and the general public.

Based on this information, the committee began designing plans for the library expansion. One of the first proposals was to implement a model based on the learning resource centre and commons models. This way, the library can support an ever-growing undergraduate population that was not considered in the original plan. With the increase in digitization, the committee also agreed that the library should have a dedicated state-of-the-art digitization centre, with specialists available both for the library and its community.

The planning committee recognized a strategic opportunity to improve the development of Colmex's digital project development by expanding library services through provision of academic systems design and development workshops for the entire campus. The library also decided to loan technological equipment including tablets, audio and video equipment, and adaptors. The library also plans to offer systems development consulting services. In order to do the latter, the library will produce a series of formalized policies and manuals for the development of digital projects. This will include digitization policies for preservation and access, workflows for maintenance and support, metadata policies, best practices and digital curation policies. In essence, we proposed what will eventually become the digital scholarship support service unit within the library.

These preliminary proposals were presented to the community by conducting an informal focus group of 15 students. Overall, the students believed that the proposed solutions were a good start and made suggestions of their own. The project committee also gave the students a guided tour to ascertain their opinions regarding the library's spaces and services. While carrying out this exercise, the committee sought information about both the use and non-use of the library. The walkthrough revealed that students felt that the library design was dated, lacked colour and was both uninviting and uncomfortable. The students confirmed that much of their work was collaborative, and that the library spaces were not conducive to that type of work. Furthermore, the group agreed that the furniture intended for individual quiet study was not suitable for long-term use. The informal group space was too close in proximity to the quiet study spaces and did not provide sufficient sound isolation. The students stated that their primary reason for utilizing the library was due to the resources and services it offered. Because of the space issues, many of the respondents entered the library only when they needed to consult materials or speak to a librarian, but rarely stayed there to work.

Additionally, the focus group respondents mentioned various national and international library projects, such as Denmark's Black Diamond library and Mexico's Vasconcelos 'megalibrary,' as examples of great libraries. They expressed a desire to have a library that (while not of that size) shares with those libraries a more modern, dynamic design and layout. The focus group sessions concluded with requests for a digital maps collection and GIS centre furnished with tactile interfaces for map plotting, visualization and interaction.

Round 2

The focus group data provided much insight into the perceptions of the student body and surprised a few of the committee members. The exercise revealed the need for a plan that would significantly transform the library in order to meet user needs. Thus, the library and the university office of development contracted two notable American consultants with expertise in planning library buildings to assist the committee and validate their plan to the university governing body and architects. Through a second series of interviews and meetings with notable members of the campus community and the architect in charge of the project (Teodoro González de León), the consultants helped formalize a plan of action that included the following:

- Understand the needs of the community.
- Outline the strategic objectives to meet user needs.
- Identify services, both current and new, which would support this strategy.
- Design spaces that would be best suited for carrying out said services.
- Specify required equipment and technology for these services.
- Determine human capital requirements (staffing, skills and capabilities).
- Produce technical documentation in conjunction with the architects and campus building and maintenance staff.

To outline user needs, the committee conducted a series of usage studies to ascertain the services and resources that the library provided to the campus. These exercises considered use of both the physical and virtual offerings of the library, including information resources, spaces and services. Studying the library's online services included the library portals and other online products, and was achieved through usability studies with Morae Usability Suite. Usage statistics were analysed with Google Analytics and by examining server logs for search terms and reference service reports. These studies revealed a pattern of increased usage of the library's online systems. Analysis of the search patterns of the library portal revealed an increasing preference for e-books and online databases. Web analytics revealed that users were increasingly utilizing mobile platforms to access library portals, results which parallel national studies of internet usage in Mexico (Asociación Mexicana de Internet, 2015).

The usage studies also examined circulation statistics and reference service reports. Observation exercises examined students' study and work habits throughout campus and demonstrated how students evolve from collaborative work in their early years of study to isolation and independent study in their later years. This could be in part due to the fact that most students are required to publish a thesis or dissertation in order to graduate from their respective programmes. This observation was contrary to the traditional notion that students tend to prefer independent study early in their studies. Much of the original library design attests to this premise. Observation also revealed that early-career students utilize spaces outside the library (such as the cafeteria or outdoor patios) for collaborative work, while upper-level and graduate work is done within the library facilities.

After reflecting on the studies' findings, the committee elaborated a strategy to pair traditional services that have characterized the library as an institution of excellence alongside new services that expand its mission and maintain its relevance both locally and among its peer institutions. With this goal in mind, a plan for comprehensive transformation was created to support new forms of interaction with digital resources, and new types of pedagogical approaches carried out on campus. The end result was the construction of spaces that adapt to the changing needs and requirements of the campus community and support distance learning, virtual and physical collaborative workflows and interweaving of device-neutral physical and digital resources.

The library's traditional, curatorial approach to acquiring pertinent physical resources is important because Latin American publishing is expected to continue producing print-only materials for the foreseeable future. Therefore, the library's expansion plan must consider an increase in shelf space. On the other hand, given the increased preference for electronic resources, we have also considered a scenario in which the library will no longer be a space for storing books, but rather for interacting and producing information. Thus, a second proposed design included the construction of a basement storage facility with high-density compact shelving.

Given that the library expansion was planned as a separate building wing, the committee devised a layout that supported students' evolving study dynamic from collaborative work to independent study. The expansion was designed with collaborative spaces on the first floor, close to the entrance. These spaces are in close proximity to the reference librarians' offices so that they are readily available to provide support. The furniture selected is highly versatile and mobile in order to facilitate teamwork and reorganization of the library space. This collaborative commons also includes various informal reading spaces and seating that foster conversation without fear of disrupting others. This replicates a cafeteria setting, one of the student focus group's preferred spaces for collaboration and conversation. The library extension design was built such that the two buildings were connected through a hallway on each floor. This design is naturally sound-isolating in such a way that the library annex will support independent study. To support electronic equipment in the library, the layout includes grid-based flush-mount electrical outlets throughout the floors.

The university IT department also created a plan to update cables for the entire network infrastructure, given its age. In order to best utilize the updated network, the committee decided to create rooms equipped with virtual conference and collaboration systems. A multimedia room was designed to assist students with the creation of audio-visual projects, such as interactive web-based documentary systems. These rooms include audio and video interfaces for recording along with web, audio and video editing software. These services tie into the equipment loaning and systems development consulting services proposed in the renovation's original iteration.

The specialized technical nature of these newer services require the library to rethink its current hiring practices. Traditionally, the library has limited itself to hiring persons with a library science background. However, due to the increasing complexity of library projects, we reconsidered this approach and now seek candidates from the greater information sciences, including interaction designers, computer programmers, communications pro-fessionals, digital preservationists and others. We hope hiring specialists from diverse academic backgrounds with a deep commitment to service, research and development will help us create library services that support local digital scholarship (Neal, 2012).

The final project plan encompassed an interior space layout based on the project architect's previous designs. The revised design included furnishings, electrical and network outlets and specific spaces (including their dimensions and explanations of their proposed use). The architect adopted the majority of these revisions. The resulting plan created spaces that adapt to the changing needs and requirements of our community. Through its design, the renovated space will support distance learning, virtual and physical collaborative workflows, and device-neutral systems that interweave physical and digital resources.

Challenges

The committee faced administrative, cultural and political challenges while planning the library reconstruction and expansion. A fundamental challenge that the group faced was the persistence of a traditional view of what a library is and does. A significant majority of the university governing body and building planners (architects, interior designers and electricians) originally planned a book-oriented solution that was limited to spaces for quiet study and increased shelving. This clashed with library personnel's objective to transform the current library into one with dynamic spaces that adapt to user needs, where people collaborate, create digital products, and make a lot of noise. The campus community's traditional view of a library caused some opposition to the project, because the community assumed the new plans would result in less use of the library and its services.

These challenges were overcome through dialogue, data-filled presentations, and interventions from the librarians and consultants. Governing body members' site visits to institutions both nationally and abroad also changed their perceptions of libraries. Institutions that they visited included Stanford University Libraries, Lemieux Library at Seattle University, the University of California Berkeley Library System, Monterrey Institute of Technology and Higher Education's Puebla Campus, and the Instituto Tecnológico Autónomo de México.

The road ahead

As this chapter was written, the clatter of the construction could be heard throughout the library. Library construction was expected to conclude in August 2015, eight months from the ground-breaking. Equipment has been purchased, and the library is slowly starting renovation, one space at a time. While this is under way, the organization itself is also beginning a transformation. For instance, at the library we are creating new positions and retraining personnel to support proposed new services. These new hires and the retraining encompass positions and skills such as electronic resources manager, digital preservation and project management. The library has also taken the initiative to increase internships, both to teach students professional skills that are absent from Mexican LIS curricula and to find staffing solutions at an economically challenging time. As a result of these internships, six digital systems have been created in-house during the same two-year period as the library renovation and expansion plan. This is due in part to the formalization of digital systems creation and the adoption of agile project planning strategies such as Scrum (an iterative planning methodology originally used in software development).

Along with this increase in systems production is a plan to create a more logical digital ecosystem. Every unit, from technical services to reference and IT, as well as the planned digital scholarship staff, are reflecting how each unit's policies, services and processes impact the overall ecosystem of the library. Everyone is working together more than ever, and so considering one unit's impact on another is imperative.

These changes, however, are only the first in a series that must eventually address the need for new types of services. These include quantitative humanistic research, text and data mining, information visualization, semantic systems development, and others. The interaction with the university governing body during this renovation has changed their perceptions of what a library should be, and has resulted in increased opportunities for the library to expand its role on campus, specifically in the development of digital information services. With this, we hope that the library space will continue to evolve with the library.

References and further reading

Arriola Navarrete, O. (2002) *Creación de un Portal: el caso de la biblioteca Daniel Cosío Villegas de El Colegio de México,* http://eprints.rclis.org/11737/1/Tesis_completa.pdf.

Asociación Mexicana de Internet (2015) *Estudio de Hábitos de los Usuarios de Internet en México,* www.amipci.org.mx/es/noticiasx/2241-alcanza-internet-el-51-de-penetracion-entre-los-usuarios-potenciales-de-mexico-amipci.

Courant, P. N. (2008) The Future of the Library in the Research University. In *No Brief Candle: reconceiving research libraries for the 21st Century,* Council on Library and Information Resources, 21–7.

Cruz, D. (2014) Clásico de Arquitectura: El Colegio de México/Abraham Zabludovksy y Teodoro González de León, *ArchDaily México,* 4 June, www.archdaily.mx/mx/02-328400/clasico-de-arquitectura-el-colegio-de-mexico-abraham-zabludovksy-y-teodoro-gonzalez-de-leon.

Cruz, D. (2015) Guía de Proyectos Mexicanos Modernos en la Expo 'Latin America in Construction' del MoMA, *ArchDaily México,* 30 March, www.archdaily.mx/mx/762108/guia-de-proyectos-mexicanos-en-la-expo-del-moma.

de León Portilla, A. H. (2012) Lingüística Mexicana. La Lingüística en la Cibernética, *Boletín del Instituto de Investigaciones Bibliográficas,* **10** (1–2).

DEFF (Denmark's Electronic Research Library) (2009) *The Future of Research and the Research Library,* www.bibliotekogmedier.dk/publikationer/artikel/the-future-of-research-and-research-library. Also at www.knowledge-exchange.info/Admin/Public/Download.aspx?file=Files%2FFiler%2Fdownloads%2FDocuments%2FReports%2FThe_Future_of_Research_and_the_Research_Library.pdf.

Dillon, A. (2008) Accelerating Learning and Discovery: refining the role of academic librarians. In *No Brief Candle: reconceiving research libraries for the 21st Century,* Council on Library and Information Resources, www.clir.org/pubs/reports/pub142/dillon.html.

Lara, L. F. (2015) Introducción, *Diccionario del Español de Mexico,* http://dem.colmex.mx/moduls/Default.aspx?id=8.

Martín, C. (2008) *Bibliotecas Universitarias: concepto y función,* Los CRAI, http://eprints.rclis.org/14816/1/crai.pdf.

McDonald, A. (2006) The Ten Commandments Revisited: the qualities of good library space, *LIBER Quarterly,* **16** (2), http://liber.library.uu.nl/index.php/lq/

article/view/7840/8010.

McMullen, S. (2008) *US Academic Libraries: today's learning commons model*, www.oecd.org/unitedstates/40051347.pdf.

Neal, J. G. (2012) *21st Century Expertise in Academic Libraries: it's all about transformation over the next decade*, www.arl.org/storage/documents/publications/ 2012-hrsym-pres-neal-j.pdf.

Peña, J. M. P. (2009) *La Alfabetización Informativa Tecnológica: estrategia fundamental en las bibliotecas del Siglo XXI*, http://aprendeenlinea.udea.edu.co/revistas/ index.php/RIB/article/view/2756/2218.

Steelcase, Inc. (2013) *Active Learning Spaces: insights, applications & solutions*, www.steelcase.com/content/uploads/sites/10/2015/03/EMEA-Insights- Guide.English.pdf.

CHAPTER 2

Researching illustrated books in art history: a brief history of the Biblioteca Digital Ovidiana project

Fátima Díez-Platas

Introduction

This chapter presents an example of a digital humanities research project created by faculty using an academic library collection. This project was developed using the Rare Books and Special Collections of Biblioteca Xeral (the main library of the University of Santiago de Compostela, Spain) to enhance art history scholarship.

Project development

When looking for a research topic in the field of art history, I discovered the rich collection of ancient and rare books of the University Library of the University of Santiago de Compostela (USC) where I am faculty. Among the library's large collection of illustrated books, two illustrated editions of the *Metamorphoses* of the Roman poet Ovid printed in Spain in the 16th century caught my attention. These two editions constituted the first objects of study and analysis, and furthermore inspired the resulting project, a study of all illustrated editions of Ovidian works (of which the USC library had a substantial collection).

Funding from the Spanish Ministry of Culture made it possible to organize a multidisciplinary research team with faculty and graduate students in the fields of art history, Latin philology and computer science from several Spanish universities (Universidad Autónoma de Barcelona, Universidad de León, Universidad de Cáceres and Universidad Pontificia de Salamanca en Madrid). The project spread from the region of Galicia (where USC is located) to Catalonia, involving three additional university libraries (Universidad de Barcelona, Universidad Pompeu Fabra in Barcelona and Universidad de Lérida). The project then spread further to the regions of Castile, León,and Madrid, providing access to prominent ancient collections at the three oldest universities in Spain: Salamanca, Complutense de Madrid and Valladolid. These various university libraries have been involved in supporting our work since 2007 when the project first began. Each library had different policies regarding the use and digitization of rare books, but overall each library's staff view OvidiusPictus (the website for the final research product) as a gateway to their collections and an additional way to share a rich Spanish bibliographic heritage.

Furthermore, this initiative's involvement with ancient illustrated books necessitated working with library special collections, an area that has historically restricted the use and manipulation of books. Our research project demanded extensive time at the library handling valuable and fragile, or sometimes already damaged, books. There were additional administrative issues regarding permission to photograph the front pages and illustrations of these books. Therefore, the assistance of the library staff and our relationship with them was indispensable to this project. The role of librarians not only facilitated our work at the library, but also created an environment of meaningful knowledge exchange for both librarians and researchers. For instance, during this project the research team acquired a deep connoisseurship of illustrated editions of Ovid, to the extent of being able to identify defective specimens that were misidentified in different libraries, increasing the accuracy within the library collections.

Rescuing ancient illustrated books for academic research

The Biblioteca Xeral at the University of Santiago de Compostela possesses an impressive rare books and special collections department of well catalogued items. However, these collections have not been completely studied and utilized for research and academic purposes. Within the collection there is a high quantity of illustrated books with many illuminations and engravings. These illustrated books constitute a real treasure for art historical research, particularly for iconographical issues (that is, interpreting the symbols, meaning and subject matter of images).

Many interesting illustrations are found in printed editions of classic works, especially different editions of the poem of *Metamorphoses* and other works by Ovid. The nature of these particular works, that is, the mythological content of the poems, prompted an extensive illustration of the mythical and legendary stories narrated by Ovid. These resulting compositions then became models for later sculptors and painters from the 15th century on. Thus, the illustrations contained in these specific books (at the Biblioteca Xeral and other academic libraries) provided an extraordinary opportunity to develop a research tool for the study of art history and specifically the iconography of mythological themes. This tool had to be digital and web-based in order to provide full and easy access to researchers.

Another positive outcome from the creation of this research tool was the diffusion of Spanish bibliographic patrimony, that is, increasing the awareness of and access to a collection that is part of a rich history of Spanish books. From this perspective, selecting, studying and processing these illustrated works by Ovid (as well as their individual illustrations) effectively rescued this library collection by making these relevant but forgotten or unknown books visible and accessible to students and researchers. Furthermore, this research also resulted in creating a new 'special collection within the special collections' that is unified by theme and period: a digital Ovidian library. Therefore, the original idea of studying mythological iconography through the illustrated editions of a particular author (Ovid) within one specific library (the Biblioteca Xeral at USC) transformed into the development of a digital research platform for the illustrated works of Ovid. Over time, the scope of this digital platform increased, and now aims to include bibliographic records for and digitized versions of all illustrations in every copy of every edition that is owned in a public or private library in Spain.

The Biblioteca Digital Ovidiana: introducing a special digital library

The Ovidian digital library (Biblioteca Digital Ovidiana, from now on BDO) is the result of the idea described above: working with the print illustrated editions of the works of Ovid, realized through an ongoing research project on Ovid, his works, and their illustrations. This library, containing bibliographic data and the results of the project, is accessible on the website OvidiusPictus (www.ovidiuspictus.es), a fully developed digital platform that is regularly adding new data and images (Díez-Platas et al., 2007–15).

Description of the project: tasks and objectives

As a long-term research project funded by the Spanish Ministry of Economy and Competitiveness, BDO is being completed in several consecutive phases. The first three phases (BDO I, BDO II and BDO III) have already been completed. The first phase, BDO I, began in 2007 and was completed in 2010, covering works held in libraries in Galicia and Catalonia that were printed between the 15th and the 19th centuries ('Biblioteca Digital Ovidiana: ediciones ilustradas de Ovidio, siglos XV-XIX (I): las bibliotecas de Galicia y Cataluña' (HUM2007-60265/ARTE)). BDO II was completed in 2012, and includes works from additional libraries in Catalonia ('Biblioteca Digital Ovidiana: ediciones ilustradas de Ovidio, siglos XV-XIX (II): las bibliotecas de Cataluña' (HAR2010-20015)). The third phase, BDO III, was completed in 2014 and includes the libraries of the autonomous community of Castile and León ('Biblioteca Digital Ovidiana: ediciones ilustradas de Ovidio, siglos XV-XIX (III): las bibliotecas de Castilla y León' (HAR2011-25853)). The fourth phase, BDO IV, is currently ongoing and planned to be completed at the end of 2016. The scope of this phase is researching Ovidian editions from the libraries of the autonomous community of Madrid ('Biblioteca Digital Ovidiana: ediciones ilustradas de Ovidio, siglos XV-XIX (III): las bibliotecas de la Comunidad de Madrid' (HAR2014-55617-P)).

The overall scope of the BDO project is the development of a digital library of Ovid's illustrated works, focusing on editions dating between the 15th and 19th centuries that are currently preserved in public and private libraries in Spain. This digital library's goal is to collocate both the bibliographic information and the iconographic study of the book illustrations in one place. As a nationwide project, the BDO aims to become a powerful instrument for scholarship on the illustrations of Ovid's works and of mythological iconography, and at the same time, act as a strong medium for disseminating Spain's bibliographic heritage.

The information contained in the BDO comes firstly from a thorough study of the illustrated editions of the works of Ovid, and secondly from the exhaustive examination of specific copies (specimens) preserved in Spanish libraries. Finally and most importantly, the BDO's information comes from the study of the books' illustrations and their iconography, which constitutes the real novelty of the research.

To achieve these results, several tasks are performed in each phase of the project:

- tracing the copies of editions of Ovidian works at the selected libraries
- individuating the illustrated specimens
- examining each illustrated specimen thoroughly (*'autopsia'*, see page 25)
- assigning a BDO identification code to each illustrated specimen (see page 25)
- creating a BDO biblio-iconographic record for each illustrated specimen
- digitizing the title page and every illustration (woodcuts and etchings) of each specimen
- studying the individuated specimens and editions
- analysing, studying and identifying the illustrations of each specimen
- processing the resulting information and data (the record and images)
- adding this data to the online OvidiusPictus database.

The project and the work at the library

The most important project tasks take place at the libraries. Tracing the existence of the works and individuating the specimens that fit the BDO's study range are the first steps, usually completed at a library. As stated before, the visual and physical inspection of every specimen is the most important task; we refer to this process by the original Greek term *autopsia*, which implies an exhaustive examination that is performed personally. Thus, the initial travel to each library and working with tangible specimens is integral to this project and cannot be replaced by a virtual exploration.

Books are individual in both story and fortune. Familiarity with each edition may be acquired through different media, but the BDO researchers' knowledge about specific specimens comes from their manipulation of and physical contact with these books. The material evidence of ancient books provides the researcher with key information about the use and observation of books, including their contents and in particular their illustrations (Dondi, 2015). Therefore, in the BDO each of the examined specimens of the illustrated editions of Ovidian works constitutes an item, an individual case and a singular piece of information that deserves particular attention and occupies its own position inside the new virtual collection formed by these Spanish copies of illustrated Ovidian editions.

Order and structure of the information: the BDO identification code and biblio-iconographic records for illustrated editions

Apart from this unique method of approaching the study of illustrated books, the BDO's primary contributions are two innovations conceived to better describe, organize and establish a knowledgeable hierarchy of the data provided by close study of these specimens:

* an identification system (code) for the specimens and editions
* a customized record format designed to display all information (bibliographic and iconographic) related to each located and examined specimen.

This identification system is based on two types of ID codes that identify items in the BDO: one code for the edition and another code for the specimen. Both codes enable better organization within the database and facilitate organization. The edition code constitutes a brief but descriptive summary of a specific edition, providing the following relevant information:

* work (*Metamorphoses, Heroides, Tristia,* etc.)
* editor
* printer
* place of publication
* date.

As an example, the *Metamorphoses* edition by Raphael Regius printed in Venice in 1493 by Simone Bevilacqua is described as: M.Regius.Bevilacqua. Venecia.1493 (or in the abbreviated version of the edition code as: M. Bevilacqua.Ven.1493). The information provided by this code unambiguously identifies each edition. The long code, being a complete description of each Ovidian illustrated edition, has become the effective 'name' identifying the edition, under which all related specimens are listed.[1]

The specimen code is a short description of the edition, copy and libraries holding that item. Each specimen code includes the following information:

- work
- acronym of the library
- place of publication
- date.

For instance, a specific copy (specimen) of the edition described in the previous example that is owned by the Biblioteca General Histórica of the University of Salamanca is described as M.BGH.Ven.1493, and a copy of the same edition that is preserved at the Biblioteca Histórica de Santa Cruz of the University of Valladolid is identified as M.BHSC.Ven.1493.

Another innovation of the BDO is a tailored record format, in the form of a table, which inventories the bibliographic and iconographic information for each specimen and edition. This 'biblio-iconographic' record describes the following information:

- title
- work
- place of publication
- printer
- patron/donor
- illustrator/engraver
- date
- edition features
- physical description of the specimen
- contents
- list of illustrations
- comments
- location
- shelfmark (call number or other information)
- record/background
- copies in Spanish libraries

- references
- bibliography.

Each BDO record includes, thus, all the usual bibliographic information (title, author and contributors, place and date of publication) and also incorporates information on the printer, patron and illustrator, linked to the corresponding records of the Consortium of European Research Libraries website (www.cerl.org). Furthermore, the record includes specific information related to the specimen, such as the physical description and comments section, which contains the annotations, *ex libris* (book provenance) and any modifications or damage.

The two most innovative and interesting parts of the record are the edition features and the list of illustrations. The edition features are divided into four subsections (text and translation, commentaries, illustration and page structure and layout) in which all the distinct features of an edition are recorded. Our aim is to encompass everything known about a particular edition, from the philological aspects (the original text, translation and commentaries, referring to all the contributors) to the more physical issues (the typeface used and the page design) and information related to the illustrative and decorative aspects (the selected set of illustrations and the antecedents of their use, the description and models of the engravings, different artists involved, etc.). The edition features faithfully reflect our expertise regarding Ovidian illustrations and the knowledge derived from the close review and study of each specimen and our iconographic analysis of individual engravings.

The list of illustrations describes each individual illustration by the edition, its location in the book, the story represented, as well as the particular circumstances affecting how each illustration appears in a particular specimen. For instance, these circumstances might include missing engravings (either removed or destroyed), bookbinding mistakes, censorship or damage.

Each BDO record is, thus, much more than a simple bibliographic record with additional information on the illustrations; it is a full research dossier with emphasis on the illustrations and their iconographic aspects. All of the information in these records is not only present in the BDO database, but also displayed on the website in a similar form. The web version of the record is more dynamic than the table layout, using expandable sections to avoid cluttering the screen with content, making the online research experience both agile and friendly. An example of this can be seen in the record for Metamorfosis.Regius.Bevilacqua.Ven.1493.[2]

Display and access to information: OvidiusPictus (the project website)

OvidiusPictus[3], the BDO project website, which launched in June 2012, features a relational database containing the aforementioned data on the specimens of illustrated editions of Ovid in Spanish libraries. Currently (in 2015), this research has been completed for libraries in Galicia, Cataluña and Castile y Leon, and has been started for Madrid libraries.

The primary contribution of this site is its carefully organized and structured information (relying on the BDO records described above) and its multiple search and access options. The layout of the site aims to facilitate searching and, therefore, the research process, offering an agile and clear platform that is still rigorous and precise. The basic structure displays information on specimens organized by century[4] or by library[5] corresponding to the main objective of the BDO project to describe illustrated Ovidian editions from the 15th to 19th century currently held in Spanish libraries. This chronological arrangement by century displays at a glance the number of specimens of illustrated editions of Ovid from each century, helping researchers determine the evolution of Ovidian editions and how his works were illustrated in different periods (although this analysis may be somewhat biased, since it only includes copies that are currently held in Spain). The arrangement by library allows researchers to visualize how many libraries own copies of illustrated Ovidian editions, how many copies are in each library, and even how many copies exist in each province and autonomous community in Spain (sorted by location).

Additionally, the search allows standard searches by title, work, place of publication or date, while adding original search fields such as printer, illustrator, and most notably by either a character within or the subject of an illustration. These original fields are specifically related to the iconographical aspects of the illustrations, enabling research on iconographic motifs, characters or episodes.[6]

Finally, the website's third contribution is a list of editions. Each edition is listed under the specific code developed to distinctly identify it. This list, like the other features described above, links each edition to the records of each specimen that is of that same edition.

A twist on the approach: the Biblioteca Digital Ovidiana and the display of book illustrations in the virtual world

The BDO project, as it has been described until this point, could be regarded as a research project on patrimony, bibliography, Classical tradition, and the reception of literary works. The BDO provides a way to achieve bibliographical expertise and a deeper knowledge about the works of Ovid and their diffusion around Europe during the 15th to the 19th centuries.

However, the fact that the books described in the BDO are *illustrated* books changes the focus of the study, and above all, changes the type of questions addressed to the gathered material. Therefore, an important innovation of the BDO project is its iconographical aspect, exploring the significance and purpose of adding images to well known texts that are themselves quite self-explanatory. The study of the illustration of each edition and specimen of Ovid's works – particularly of the *Metamorphoses*, which are the most important reservoir of mythological material in Western literature – leads to an exploration of the function of illustrated texts and how illustrations have evolved over time. The *BDO*, then, is not only a patrimonial and bibliographic project, but also an iconographical one. Moreover, the approach taken with the BDO to analyse and display ancient illustrated books provides an extraordinary opportunity for further research in art history, iconography and mythological studies.

The digitization of the entire illustrative content of each book creates an interesting research opportunity in art history, particularly related to the implications of the choices made when displaying these images. On the one hand, the information in each specimen's record entails a virtual process of actually 'dismembering' the book to extract its iconographic information. On the other hand, the creation of online image galleries[7] for each book allows the viewer to comprehend the whole figurative version of the text in an almost immediate way, a phenomenon unique to images. This simple device used to display digital images – comparable to the results of a Google image search – lets us reflect on the relationship between the display of the images and the perception of the information of the book, and its implications.

Illustrated books are full of images that accompany, explain, or 'translate in images' their textual content. All the illustrations within a book are submitted to the book structure by virtue of their attachment to the text itself. This structure and the requirements of the page force us to approach the illustrations in the same way as the text, that is, consecutively, subject to the linear sequence of time. Book illustrations thus acquire some textual qualities, or to be more clear, I would say that images within illustrated books acquire 'bookish' qualities. These bookish qualities include time and sequence; every image is compelled to be observed on its page, along with the text that accompanies it in the physical space of the page. The illustration is often inseparable from the textual content that explains it, or *vice versa*. Thus the images must of necessity be understood in the environment of the book, which implies a page-by-page rhythm.

On the other hand, the book illustrations rely on the ability of the image as a medium to convey information in a specific way that entails a certain amount of immediacy and simultaneity. Furthermore, the illustrations within a book are related to each other by the unity and narrative sequence of the text that they illustrate. They constitute a visual corpus, a collection that constitutes a coherent whole. The illustrations make up a sort of iconographic cycle that demands being perceived together. This is particularly true in the case of a mythological book like the *Metamorphoses* (though also in other works of Ovid), because the illustrations share the same relationship as the intertwined stories of the poem. However, as has been explained above, because images within a book are submitted to sequence and time through their position and display within that book, the link between the images is not easy to perceive. In other words, the physical restrictions of book illustrations make a complete and simultaneous comprehension of the entire illustration series impossible.

Another way to understand this idea is that illustrations provide a completely different way of conveying the content of a book; they create something like a 'parallel universe' hiding behind the illustrated book. The only way to enter this universe would be to destroy the book, detach its pages, choose the illustrated pages and set them in order one beside each other, as in the *Musee imaginaire* of André Malraux. How can we move from sequence to simultaneity, without actually dismembering the illustrated book?

Only the digital world enables us to perform such a transformation of the illustrated book. Within the virtual reality of the BDO, by digitizing each illustration and by setting them together, the complete figurative story of the book becomes reality. The whole illustrative programme can be perceived together; moreover, the sequence of the illustrations' story can be reconstructed, following a different time: the time of images. Within this digital realm, the researcher is able to perform the primary functions of art history: establish relationships, compare images, spot similarities and differences, and detect underlying ties between them.

Obviously, this process also implies a de-contextualization of the image, similar to the way that pictures or objects in a museum are removed from their original context. Nevertheless, in the BDO, the images are not completely decontextualized, because they are still linked to the bibliographic record, so they are still part of the book. Therefore, one of the most interesting aspects of displaying this whole corpus of illustrations is the coherence that lies behind it, which is partly conferred by the entity of the book itself. By constructing digital image galleries, we enter into the question of format, because this digital medium enables a transformation of the sequential formation of the illustrated book into a simultaneous board of images: the thumbnail gallery.

This change of format that collocates images and sets them side by side can be compared to two different processes related to the display of museum objects. First, this represents a process of de-contextualization similar to what happens to the elements of a cyclical image when displayed in a museum or exhibition. For instance, the metopes of the series of the twelve labours of Herakles (Hercules), despite being detached from the temple to which they belonged, continue to be strongly bonded by the coherence of the corpus that they compose. Second, the change of format performed by constructing a digital gallery or board of images grouped together could be considered as the inverse process of constructing a museum or exhibition catalogue. Making a museum catalogue transforms the pictures hanging together on the walls of the museum gallery into illustrations tied to a text within a book.

To conclude, the images contained in the BDO, which are the digitized engravings that illustrated various editions of Ovidian works, create a kind of virtual museum filled with different galleries. This method of displaying and consequently of analysing the images of illustrated books in the BDO offers a unique opportunity to perform art history and iconographic research within the library. Last, but not least, this virtual approach enables the performance of digital research, and creating actual digital art history, because the BDO transforms each digitized specimen of an illustrated edition into a specific virtual museum of the contents of that book. Thus, this material that was once confined to the rare books and special collections areas of many libraries in Spain can now be researched and explored through digital means with a new visual perspective.

References

Díez-Platas, F., Gonzales Castiñeiras, M.A., Meilan Jacome, P., Morales Moran, J., García Nistal, J, Garcia Gomez, E., Fernandez Paz, M. et al. (2007–15) OvidusPictus, www.ovidiuspictus.es. Also available at www.ovidiuspictus.eu and www.ovidiuspictus.net.

Dondi, C. (2015) *Material Evidence in Incunabula*, Consortium of European Research Libraries (CERL), www.cerl.org/resources/mei/main.

Websites

1 List of editions, www.ovidiuspictus.es/listadoediciones.php.
2 Record for Metamorfosis.Regius.Bevilacqua.Ven.1493, www.ovidiuspictus.es/visualizacionejemplar.php?clave=122%20&%20clave1=M.BGH.Ven.1493.
3 OvidiusPictus homepage, www.ovidiuspictus.es/.
4 Centuries of preserved specimens (navigation), www.ovidiuspictus.es/siglos.php.
5 Municipality and library navigation page, www.ovidiuspictus.es/bibliotecascomunidades.php.

6   Search function (by iconographic motif, character or episode), www.ovidiuspictus.es/busquedabasica.php.
7   Gallery of images from Metamorfosis.Regius.Mazzali.Parma.1505i, http://bit.ly/1NLklTM.

CHAPTER 3

The 'Developing Librarian' digital scholarship pilot training project

Richard Freeman

In February 2014 a group of library faculty, curators, and staff at the University of Florida (UF) Smathers Libraries formed the Digital Humanities Library Group (DHLG). The group was to be a reading group to discuss issues on digital scholarship (DS), including the state of DS in the UF libraries.[1] Members also had the intention to put the theory into practice. The group began with an invitation to librarians and staff. Twenty-six responded, the majority of whom were library faculty. The first few meetings were well attended, with over a dozen attendees. Within six months, a training project intended to give us new DS skills was created, a mini-grant was procured and the 'Developing Librarian' digital scholarship pilot training project began. This paper will use ethnographic methods – participant observation, surveys and interviews with individual participants – to tell the narrative of this project: how and why it started, what goals and aspirations the participants have, and how they evaluated it. As I write this, we are in the 11th month of the 12-month grant. Most participants agree that the project will continue after the grant officially ends. While a definitive assessment cannot yet be made, every group has nearly completed their respective projects and everyone agrees that we have learned a great deal.

In the beginning

The DHLG Developing Librarian Project benefits us all by bringing us together as a community of practice, having us all learn together and learn to work together, and having us be seen as equals and collaborators with our teaching faculty.

Respondent to survey question on how the project benefits the libraries[2]

In the beginning there was the University's 'Data Management and Curation Task Force,' co-chaired by Laurie Taylor, the library's Digital Scholarship Librarian. Blake Landor, our Classics, Philosophy and Religion librarian, was asked to serve on it, and he agreed, 'without really knowing what I was getting myself into' (Landor, 2015a). Landor soon questioned his own place in this group: 'I felt a little out of place on that committee, it was dominated by people in sciences, understandably . . . not much of the discussion dealt with things that I was directly involved in' (Landor, 2015b). The committee drafted a document listing a set of skills recommended for librarians to have, 'but a good many of those guidelines it seemed to me were irrelevant for . . . digital humanities' (*ibid.*). After a discussion with Taylor, Landor wrote a proposal to the library administration to formally recognize a library group dedicated to digital scholarship and approve release time for its members. One of the selling points was that the English and History departments were discussing creating a certificate programme in the digital humanities, and it was believed by Landor, Taylor and others that the libraries should be skilled in working with the faculty and students in this programme. The original group Landor proposed was a small group of faculty librarians, but the administration suggested it be opened up to the wider library community, and change its then-proposed name, 'The Digital Caucus'. And thus was born 'The Digital Humanities Library Group' or DHLG, with Landor as chair.

To write the proposal, Landor read digital scholarship literature. One of the group's first tasks was to read and discuss these and other articles. Some articles were from a 2013 volume of the *Journal of Library Administration*. The issue is dedicated to discussions on digital scholarship (DS) and how it is redefining librarians' roles and relationships with faculty and researchers (Rockenbach, 2013). Some salient issues covered in these articles include a mention of Columbia University's 'reskilling' librarians project, the University of Maryland's semester-long DS workshops for librarians (Posner, 2013) and the need for retraining in general (Rockenbach, 2013). Others discuss the possibilities of being a true collaborator with faculty, not merely 'support', and more practical examples of models used in libraries – with a reference to an earlier piece by Vandegrift, to just jump in and do it (Nowviskie, 2013; Vandegrift and Varner, 2013; Vandegrift, quoted in Sula, 2013). There are many processes involved with DS projects, and many are very technical, so it can be near-paralysing to get started. Several authors attempt to stop this paralysis, suggesting that one should not dwell too much on obstacles and just start a project, any project. No one is an expert on all things digital, so begin with one or two processes needed to accomplish a specific project.

As to the 'novel' idea of librarians as partners with other faculty, and not merely support staff, Nowviskie (2013) points out how many librarians currently have PhDs and second master's degrees and are quite capable of taking on research projects on their own, and thus also partnering with other faculty across campus. Nowviskie indicated a possible stumbling block: the small percentage of time that librarian appointments typically designate for scholarship. At Nowviskie's institution, the University of Virginia, research makes up 20% of a librarian's appointment, while at the University of Florida (UF) it is only 10%. This contrasts markedly with teaching and research faculty, who face the pressures of 'publish or perish.' Another obstacle, I might add, is that many faculty do not think to ask librarians to partner with them. This is not for lack of respect, but due to a lack of knowledge of our backgrounds and abilities. But this topic is for another paper.[3]

Landor became intrigued with the librarian reskilling project at Columbia University. As the DHLG was a self-selected group, no one questioned digital scholarship's important role in research or the potential for librarians to play a central role in its growth. What was missing was the skill set, experience and opportunities for librarians. Thus, at a meeting in March 2014, we decided to start our own training project. One member explained hopes for the experience this way: 'I am interested in the humanities. I wanted to get some exposure to tools and techniques being used in the digital humanities. Depending on how much I learn and on my regular job duties, I thought I might be able to assist digital humanities researchers in the future.' A few group members mentioned an interest in specific aspects of DS, such as text mining or GIS. Everyone in the group hoped to learn new skills. One modest goal is simply to understand the scope of the tools currently being used and to be able to have an intelligent conversation with someone asking for advice about starting a DS project. As one member stated, 'I wanted to better understand what digital humanities projects were about and what programs and what theories it entailed'. And another was very direct in wanting to learn what tools are being used in order to point patrons in the right direction, for instance, 'Use x program if you want to do y project.' In sum, while no one expects to be an expert in these programs, we all hope to gain a familiarity with them and to understand not only their significance in DS, but also what DS looks like in practice.

The first order(s) of business

I think everyone is learning, which is the prime goal of the project. There might be some disgruntled people due to a lack of structure as a large group. Learning about working in groups is also a learning curve.

Respondent to survey question asking for general observations

With agreement on our new path, the next item was to choose a project. We did not lack for ideas, which ranged from digitizing and creating a website for art books, scrapbooks from the Popular Culture collection and a section of materials on segregation from the Florida Subject Files. The second most popular idea was to digitize a part of a larger collection of World War 1 sheet music. All these projects involve collection enhancements and training in technologies such as linked data, GIS, TEI, text mining and online exhibits. The chosen project was to enhance part of an already-digitized collection, the Brothers Grimm Digital Collection (part of the Baldwin Library of Historical Children's Literature).

We chose the Brothers Grimm project after realizing that digitizing materials is not an important aspect of research. It is a mechanical process that is not overly complex and is very time-consuming. Working with an already-digitized collection allowed us to dive right into learning new skills. The project was suggested by Suzan Alteri, the curator of the Baldwin collection. This was not completely altruistic; Alteri hoped that it would 'help me as a curator . . . it seemed like the group could do a really great online exhibit . . . to provide context to the sub-collection that was created out of the digitized materials for the [physical] exhibit [displayed earlier], and allow us to do some TEI coding . . . for text mining' (Alteri, 2015). Alteri did feel a little protective and had doubts about using 'her' collection as a guinea pig on more than one occasion. 'On the one hand I'm a project participant,' she stated, 'on the other hand I'm the curator of the Grimm sub-collection that we're using. . . . Those two roles often, I found now, compete with each other. . . . I had the voice in my head that was the project participant and then this voice in my head that said, "wait a minute, what do they want to do to that?"' It was sometimes a bit stressful for Alteri to play both roles.

Once the project was decided, we asked Bess de Farber, our grant and project management expert, to talk to us. She suggested we apply for one of the library's internal mini-grants. With the deadline arriving soon, we had to rush the process. Landor was the primary grant writer, with help from Taylor and comments and suggestions by team members, including myself. This was a great way to concretize the project. Here is a passage from the grant:

a) Project Description

This Mini Grant will support the training sessions and activities needed for actualizing a digital humanities project as part of the larger effort to create a model for building capacity for future ongoing growth of digital humanities activities centered in the Libraries. . . .

The completion of this project and training program will not only add value to a prized collection, but it will build a human infrastructure of skilled Digital Humanities practitioners and consultants in Smathers Libraries. Participants in this Mini Grant, many of whom lack experience with digital humanities tools and projects, will develop a number of skills, including GIS/Data visualization; online portfolio development; project design with project charters and collaborative practices; project management concepts and skills; text encoding and use of metadata; and online exhibit design . . .

Digital Humanities Library Group, 2014a, 3

As a part of the grant application, each member wrote a letter of commitment, promising 10 hours a month to be devoted to the project (6% of our work time). Funds were requested to pay for outside experts to lead workshops and for a graduate student (familiar with DS software) to assist us throughout the year. The total amount of money requested was US$4993 (the grant limit was US$5000).

With the grant awarded, and before any work began, Taylor suggested we create a project charter. She explained that charters are helpful for establishing an agreed-upon timeline, defining group roles, crediting work done about the project, and for providing group 'buy-in' for the project through their participation in its planning and implementation. As Taylor puts it,

> You want the group to feel ownership of the project . . . involvement . . . and what they are committing to. I have a lot of project management experience . . . the single biggest problem that people run into is the people . . . communication . . . having everyone create a shared document where they commit to what they believe the project is for, how they believe it's going to work. . . . It's a tough process, it's the first group communication . . . but [being only a charter] it takes some of the stress level down and so people can work through some of those interpersonal dynamics . . . and the group can come together as a group.
>
> Taylor, 2015

On 3 September 2014 Taylor and fellow-librarian Michelle Leonard kicked things off with a workshop that explained charters and their value. They noted that when projects go wrong, problems are often caused by:

- Unclear goals
- Disagreement about goals
- Scope is unconstrained (too much, too open)
- Disagreement on roles (who does what)
- Inadequate resources/staffing
- Disagreements, resentments, burn out.

Leonard and Taylor, 2014

These were among the main issues we set forth to tackle. Further discussion was set for 22 September, when we wrote a first draft of the charter. We finalized the draft in a meeting on 1 October (a self-imposed deadline). Successfully meeting this first deadline was greeted with enthusiasm and high-fives all around. The project was named: 'Mining the Brothers Grimm: Curating a Digital Subcollection'. When writing the charter it was sometimes confusing to keep the objectives of this project separate from those of the 'Developing Librarian' training project. According to the charter,

> The team will create an online exhibit and engage in digital curation activities to enhance the scholarly context of, and add value to, the digitized Brothers Grimm subcollection. We will employ digital curation skills acquired during the year-long 'Developing Librarian' Digital Humanities Pilot Training mini-grant. The grant supports training to enhance library collaboration on digital scholarship. Successful completion of the *Mining the Brothers Grimm* project will be evidence of our learning process.
>
> Digital Humanities Library Group, 2014b, 1

The Brothers Grimm project provides a context in which to test our newly acquired skills, the purpose of the 'Developing Librarian' training project. In addition to the training sessions, groups meet semi-regularly, and everyone has individual tasks assigned in their work group.

Getting it done: training, work groups and the work

> Developing relationships with others not in my department. I got exposure to different digital tools, even tho' I don't necessarily understand what they are and what they can do.

> [It] has been exciting to get more concrete exposure to the kinds of tools and projects that are out there. It has been a good collaborative experience in general. I've learned several important new things and have a better sense of the field.

The above quotes nicely express the overall sentiments of the group and the value found in the activities, training sessions and interactions that we have all experienced. Another participant enjoyed 'listening and learning in the group setting', touching on a positive experience as part of a learning community. This positive aspect was mentioned by several team members, including this comment: 'It's impressive to see the level of curiosity and openness that my colleagues in this project have'. It is these two topics, the training sessions and working groups, which I will discuss in this section.

Working groups

> Seeing how excited people are, and how ready people are to learn, grapple with
> big and small issues and do and make things!
>> Respondent to survey question on the most positive things experienced

With so much work to be done, we broke it down into tasks. These tasks revolved around four activities, so we created four groups. Everyone was required to join one group, although you could join more if you wished, or simply sit in on any group meetings. Three groups were the 'TEI Working Group', the 'Exhibit Working Group' and the 'DHLG Studio Working Group'. The fourth group was charged with creating a project blog for group updates and personal musings about the project. I was in this group and learned how to set up and manage a blog using WordPress. Once the blog was set up, it required little maintenance, and so I also chose to participate in the TEI group.

There are two project deliverables for the Brothers Grimm project. One is to enhance a digital copy of the first English translation of *Kinder und Haus Märchen* (Children and Household Tales), titled 'German Popular Stories' (Grimm, 1823). By coding the entire volume using the Text Encoding Initiative's (TEI) guidelines, participants will enhance scholarly access to this important translation. Text encoding entails manually adding mark-up language (html-like codes) to texts so that they are machine-readable. With full texts encoded, one can create an algorithm to locate and count specific terms or phrases in a text, and to search for changes in language which may denote historical importance, such as a shift in cultural perception of that object/phenomenon. Books are often scanned as images of pages (TIFFs) and thus do not allow for machine-readable searching. TEI allows the computer to present the pages in a way that closely resembles that of the original publication (line breaks, section headings, etc.). To do this, group members learned how to code using TEI and the XML editor program oXygen, which also checks for errors in the coding. Chapters and sections of the book were divided among the group. The group also used Boilerplate, which allows you to view your work as it will appear online.

The second deliverable is an online exhibit of the Brothers Grimm tales. The exhibit examines issues such as truth and myths, German history and political thought, and national identities. Exhibits attract the general public and researchers, so this is both a research source in its own right and provides publicity for the greater Baldwin Library collection. In the group's initial meeting there was general consensus to use the Omeka platform to learn layout and design and produce an exhibit for the Brothers Grimm digital sub-collection website. They also wished to learn Neatline, a suite of geo-temporal exhibition building tools (plug-ins) for Omeka. The group decided to concentrate the exhibit on one tale, 'Cinderella'. The vision for the exhibit is a home page with content on various aspects of the tale housed in separate modules so that more can be added at a later date, perhaps tying it to the TEI-encoded text in some way.

The fourth group created the digital scholarship lab, which was not something we originally planned as part of this project. It is tangential to the Brothers Grimm project, but central to the DHLG as a whole. In March 2014 the idea for a space in the libraries dedicated to digital scholarship was discussed in a DHLG meeting. That same week, a group member read about the then-new Digital Scholarship Lab at Brown University. This information was sent to the entire DHLG listserve, which included our Dean, Judy Russell. One day later, we received this message from Dean Russell: 'How big a space would we need – and what equipment – to establish a lab like this here at UF? Could library faculty teach such a course or team teach it with faculty from one of the colleges?' (Taylor, 2015). From there we were off and running. We did not have the same funds as Brown University, so we took a minimalist approach. We were offered a very prominent room in the library and were funded to purchase two large screens (one a touch screen), a new projection system and three computers with appropriate software. We also found furniture more conducive to working in small groups to replace individual classroom desks. We painted one wall with chalkboard paint – another wall is glass, so dry markers can be used. Our goal was to create a space that would encourage creative thought and play. On 16 March 2015 we held the opening for the Scott Nygren Scholars Studio (http://cms.uflib.ufl.edu/librarywest/studio).[4] Although it is 'open,' there are still issues to be worked out, such as hours and staffing.

Training

> The most positive experience has been the trainings. In many I learn new skills and in those I do not have a strong background in or do not understand as well (GIS for example), I do at least learn an understanding of why people use a particular tool and how they use it.

> With very few exceptions, the training sessions have been of high quality and practical.

Neither the TEI project nor the online exhibit would have been possible without training. Training, after all, was the prime purpose of this entire enterprise. The group projects were merely to practise what we learn. If we can finish them, great. If they are useful, even better. But regardless, if we learn, it is a successful project. Thus, grant funds primarily funded specialists who led hands-on workshops. For some skills we called on our own experts.

From August 2014 to April 2015 we held 18 workshops. The kick-off was 12 August 2014 with Alex Gil, who helped organize the Columbia University librarian training project that inspired us. Guests from within UF and the libraries led workshops on GIS/visualization training, metadata training, data mining and online exhibit training. Our local experts mainly came from the libraries but included a graduate student from the English department and a grant-funded graduate assistant. Our other two outside presenters were Syd Bauman (on TEI and text mark-up) and Scott Weingart (on data visualization).

A critical summing up
The good

Generally participants enjoyed working in groups, though for some it was a learning experience. One participant summed it up very nicely:

> The most important thing that we are learning is not technical. It's how to work together as a group, to encourage fluidity but to learn to set boundaries. To inculcate flexibility – even as we make sure is equity [sic]. Often, lack of rigid roles leads to an uneven distribution of work. We are learning how to manage that social aspect of learning new technologies.

Below are two comments that nicely summarize the project's benefits for the community and the individual:

> This benefits the libraries as a whole because we now have a corpus of knowledge that we can use to collaborate with students and faculty on digital humanities projects and we can also use this in our own research.

> I will be familiar with what can be done in digital humanities, maybe gain some experience in doing simple projects myself. And can – to some extent – advise faculty on how to 'do' DH. Perhaps can also begin my own projects.

Needs work

Considering its length and logistics, there is no way a project like this will not hit some bumps. What many of us have realized, however, is that these bumps are also a part of the learning experience. The most common critiques from project participants are two related issues: time constraints and planning. Several participants lamented that we lost focus by emphasizing the deliverables more than the learning process itself. However, many participants remarked throughout the spring that if the project ended that day, it would be successful because of what we learned. Finally, while the instruction was excellent, some felt a bit lost after the speaker left. This also ties into time constraints. One member suggested:

> Go/start slower, smaller more concrete steps. Clearer goals (and, again, smaller). More group presentations of our progress as we go along. I know I am frustrated because I don't feel I am prepared to do the duties I was assigned, and we have no resources for me to go to (which is what we are supposed to become ourselves).

Several participants suggested that this could have been a two-year project: 'I would have preferred a schedule that concentrated purely on training throughout the first year (with some repeat and more in-depth sessions) and then moving on to executing a project in a second year.' As discussed, there are two deliverables. The library has an in-house expert on online exhibits, but there is no local TEI expert. This was frustrating for the TEI group, as TEI is an extremely meticulous, time-consuming language to learn, without an easy online guide. We often felt ill-prepared to perform our assigned tasks. Finally, as one of the blog creators, I wish it had been better utilized as a real community bulletin board. I would like to research how to better integrate a blog for a learning community.

Some final thoughts

While all of the above criticisms are on the mark, they are best viewed in perspective with the pace in which this project grew from an idea to reality. The first idea for this project began in March 2014. A grant was discussed in April, with a deadline in May. The idea for the scholars' studio came up in March, and two days later we were asked to immediately write a proposal. By June, we were making plans for the grant, which began in July. Our first guest speaker came in August, before we even thought of the charter. With the current state of our deliverables, the scholars' studio open, and 18 presentations later, it is an amazing accomplishment. This was all done by a group of 14 librarians and staff. A participant who critiqued the instructional levels nonetheless believes the project was 'Very worthwhile. A bit ambitious', and then concludes: 'Group learning and building relationships as a result of teamwork on projects is a wonderful experience – wish we could do more. It is very rewarding (unlike the usual group committee work we do).'

This project has opened doors for several of our members, even though the project is not yet complete. Three members organized a panel about the project for the Florida Association of Academic Libraries (FACRL), others presented their experiences at the Florida THAT Camp in Orlando, and I have written this chapter. Aaron Beveridge, the English graduate student who presented to us on MassMine, worked with several group members and was awarded a US$60,000 NEH grant to complete the development of the software.[5]

If we were to start today with what we know now, what might that look like? As a participant myself, I would appreciate a longer time frame, but I do not know if the suggestion to have workshops first, then start the project, would be wise. I believe our strategy to learn while we work on a project makes sense, but I would emphasize that it is the learning process itself, not the final projects, that is important. This strategy might have brought the stress level down a notch for some group members. Perhaps we could keep this format and lengthen the project. As it is, we will be working on it past the grant deadline of 30 June 2015. Other than these wrinkles, everyone agrees that the project was successful and valuable. My advice for librarians in other institutions who are interested in similar projects recalls my earlier paraphrasing of Vandegrift: just do it![6]

References

Alteri, S. (2015) Personal interview, 31 March.

Digital Humanities Library Group (2014a) *Smathers Libraries Mini Grant Proposal: 'Developing Librarian' digital humanities pilot training project,* http://ufdc.ufl.edu/AA00022054/00001?search=brothers+=grimm.

Digital Humanities Library Group (2014b) *Project Charter, Mining the Brothers Grimm: curating a digital subcollection,* http://ufdc.ufl.edu/AA00022054/00012?search=project+=charter+=grimm.

Grimm, M. M., ed. (1823) *German Popular Stories: translated from the Kinder und Haus Märchen, collected by M. M. Grimm, from oral tradition,* London, UK, C. Baldwin, publisher.

Landor, B. (2015a) Personal correspondence, 26 March.

Landor, B. (2015b) Personal interview, 26 March.

Leonard, M. and Taylor, L. (2014) *Project Charters and Prenups for Scientists: UF Digital Humanities Library Group training,* presentation given at Smathers Libraries, University of Florida, Gainesville, 3 September.

Nowviskie, B. (2013) Skunks in the Library: a path to production for scholarly R&D, *Journal of Library Administration,* **53**, 53–66.

Pasek, J. E. (2015) Organizing the Liaison Role: a concept map, *College and Research Libraries News,* **76** (4), 202–5.

Posner, M. (2013) No Half Measures: overcoming common challenges to doing digital humanities in the library, *Journal of Library Administration,* **53**, 43–52.

Rockenbach, B. (2013) Introduction, *Journal of Library Administration,* **53**, 1–9.

Sula, C. A. (2013) Digital Humanities and Libraries: a conceptual model, *Journal of Library Administration,* **53**, 10–26.

Taylor, L. (2015) Personal interview, 8 April, 8.

Vandegrift, M. and Varner, S. (2013) Evolving in Common: creating mutually supportive relationships between libraries and the digital humanities, *Journal of Library Administration*, **53**, 67–78.

Notes

1   While the term used in most of the literature is 'digital humanities' I prefer the more inclusive term of 'digital scholarship' (DS). This may be partly due to the fact that I am a trained social scientist. I feel strongly that using the term 'humanities' may be a barrier to attracting practitioners in other disciplines. It is easy to decide not to attend an event that excludes us (and others) in its title. This is a shame because the processes involved in DS are relevant to research in many disciplines.

2   All quotes in this chapter that are not attributed to a specific individual were taken from an anonymous online survey I sent out to members of the group. My response rate was 70%.

3   I might add that I have been asked by faculty in my discipline to work with them, and have approached faculty outside my discipline to work on projects, and have been welcomed. So this is not an insurmountable problem (c.f. Pasek 2015).

4   Scott Nygren was the Director of the Center for Film and Media Studies, and a Professor in the Department of English. He was a strong booster for the libraries. He passed away due to cancer in 2014.

5   The grant title is: 'MassMine: collecting and archiving big data for social media humanities research.' The grant is posted at: http://ufdc.ufl.edu/AA00025642/00001.

6   I would like to thank everyone on the DHLG team, with special thanks to Blake Landor, Suzan Alteri, Laurie Taylor and Missy Clapp.

PART 2

Data services and data literacy

Introduction to Part 2

Jackie Carter

If data is 'the lifeblood of research', it follows that importance must be placed upon the skills and services required to use this asset in support of the pursuit of new knowledge (Paul Boyle, as cited in Economic and Social Research Council, 2012). At a time when we can barely go a day without encountering another invitation to an event on big data, or come across an article on insight to be drawn from data big or small, there has arguably never been a better time to think about the practice of data analysis and the need for data literacy. In the UK we are fortunate to have investment at the national level in data services, including the flagship UK Data Service, to enable social science and related researchers to discover and use data that has been collected for the purpose of social research. However the practice of research data management (RDM), data literacy and data skills is spread widely across the academy. From the undergraduate student using secondary data in their final-year dissertation to the experienced researcher collecting primary data in the field, from the small organization starting to collect data to inform their day-to-day decisions to corporates who rely on data for insight into their business strategies, research data management practices can and should be taught as part of a skill set much needed, and increasingly valued, by society.

Data is not new. Good research has always relied on good data as a starting point. What is emerging, however, is a new profession being described, sometimes quite loosely, as data science. Clearly researchers across the disciplines have always managed their data, in ways that have enabled them to contribute to the scholarly debate and literature in their subject areas. What is less evident, except perhaps in some of the hard sciences, is the documentation of the data and methods underpinning this research. How was the data derived, what methods were used, what was included and excluded, what version of data is being used in the study? All these questions, and others, need to be considered before even starting to analyse the data. A good data literacy programme will start with these fundamental questions. There is, of course, however much more to understanding data than these simple questions.

The widely cited McKinsey 2011 Report makes much of the need to develop data services and skills (Manyika et al., 2011). Notwithstanding that the focus of this report was on big data and business, the apparent need for the data infrastructure and analytical skill set to be developed to exploit the rise of data is evident throughout. The increase in the number of Data Analytics degree programmes testifies to the increased value being placed by universities on the data-driven focus of current and future research. The University of California at Berkeley provides an example of such a Data Analytics programme; as its website states, 'The field of data science is emerging at the intersection of the fields of social science and statistics, information and computer science, and design' (UC Berkeley School of Information, 2015).

By definition, then, data science is a cross-disciplinary area. The chapters within this section focus on the skills required to critically evaluate data sources, as well as on the development of methods for, and the practice of, data analysis. The case has been presented for why this is an emerging field. Let us next consider the importance associated with learning the skills to appreciate and practise research data analysis in the development of becoming professionals in whichever field we are in, or our students move into, and how libraries and data services can support this endeavour.

The chapters in this section reflect on data services developing in support of students' and researchers' needs. Much has been happening in the UK in this area in recent years. Indeed, the UK has invested centrally in development of research data management support services and the creation of resources that can be shared, wherever possible, openly in a strategic attempt to tackle the need for improved access to, discovery of, creation and use of research data. The UK Jisc Research Data Management blog (Jisc, 2015) captures the activity in this area since the development of the RDM programme in 2011, whilst the Digital Curation Centre provides access to resources to assist those developing RDM services, including resources specifically for librarians (Digital Curation Centre, 2004–15). Another service, Jorum, supporting access to open educational resources, provides collections of Creative Commons-licensed resources for both RDM and data and information and digital literacy skills (Jisc, n.d.). Meanwhile, a 2014 textbook, *Managing and Sharing Research Data: a guide to good practice*, has been instrumental in contributing to the data professional's toolkit in this emerging field by collecting examples of good practice of research data management practices developed over many years at the UK Data Archive (Corti et al., 2014; Grundy, 2014).

A national programme in the UK called Q-Step, initiated in 2013 and set to run for 10 years, is explicitly funded to support the development of data-literate graduates. Social science courses at UK universities, economics majors aside, are not producing graduates with the skill set to critique or make sense of numeric data, nor to use data in undertaking research. The result is a 'skills gap' in the labour market of quantitatively trained social science graduates and a poor supply of graduates to take up careers in social research or quantitative disciplines. The UK Q-Step initiative is a strategic attempt to redress this balance (Nuffield Foundation, 2015).

Fifteen UK universities won funding through Q-Step to begin to create a step change in quantitative social science training. The programme is designed to be experimental, with the main criterion for success being to introduce 'additionality' within the universities involved, but in time across higher education and beyond. As a consequence, each centre has a slightly different approach, with the 15 collectively exploring new and innovative ways of teaching data analysis through specialist new curricula and extending the skills learned to the workplace through work placements and internships. The resulting expertise and resources developed will be shared widely across the higher education sector, in the UK and overseas (where permissions allow). Importantly, links with schools and employers will be developed to give attention to the pipeline of social science data students in regard to where they will come from, to study quantitative social science at university, and where they will go to once they graduate.

At the University of Manchester our aims are twofold. First, we plan to raise the bar for all undergraduate students by embedding quantitative data analysis in the classroom, in substantive teaching across the social sciences. By doing this we expect to make more students aware of the value of quantitative data for social research, and to support development of the skills to critique data and their sources, use data in their own research projects, and in time become data producers. Developing future quantitative social researchers also underpins this approach. Our experiences of embedding data in the classroom are shared through case studies (Buckley et al., 2015). Secondly, we plan to give more students opportunities to see how data is used in the real world, in research and decision-making and in policy formation. We do this by running a paid internship scheme across the summer of the second year (typically the middle year of a three-year degree programme). Places are competitive; students apply and if successfully shortlisted are interviewed by a member of the Q-Step team and the organization offering the placement. In 2014, the pilot year, 19 students were placed in two UK cities, in think-tanks, universities (planning and research departments), market research companies and polling organizations, as well as local government departments. In 2015 more than 40 students gained data-driven employment experience in five cities, in organizations ranging from banks, international statistical organizations (the World Bank), think-tanks, market research groups, social research consultancies, national and local government departments, news and media companies, charities and small businesses.

Employability is a big driver in universities in these times. Students worldwide increasingly graduate with large debts, and in the UK this is particularly the case in recent years as a consequence of changing government policy and increased tuition fees, as seen in a recent UK report on student loan debt that features international comparisons (Bolton, 2015). Our students and employers are therefore searching for evidence of graduate employable skills. The Q-Step programme is enabling us to capture evidence of these skills from the students' and employers' perspectives.

In order to showcase the benefits of this workplace learning we developed six short films. A promotional film highlights the experiences of four of our students at the University of Manchester who worked across a number of organizations (School of Social Sciences, 2015). Their experiences included acquiring experience of collecting data (including submitting their own questions to a panel for YouGov political and social polling), an in-depth data analysis for progression and retention of students at the University of Manchester, working for a social action think-tank, and developing a pamphlet for industry and government on the evidence base for the third runway at Heathrow airport from the voice of the traveller. Although just eight weeks in length, the internships provided students with sufficient time to put the skills they had learned in the classroom into practice in a variety of ways. Individual films of five of the Q-Step students were also created and have been shared on YouTube (School of Social Sciences, n.d.).

The students participating in these internships are all paid a living wage. The work is not credit-bearing; that is, it does not count towards their degree. Nonetheless, it provides an excellent opportunity to understand the world of social research. Our interviews with students following their placements have also revealed the value they place on this opportunity, and the benefits they experienced as a result, as demonstrated by the selection of quotes below.

My placement was great – I really enjoyed it! I was glad for the experience as it's helped me with my CV and with interviews. I definitely feel more employable – I have since secured a job as a Research Assistant for a search engine company here in Manchester.

Pete Jones, Manchester City Council Q-Step Summer Placement 2014 Student

I loved my placement! We got on really well – for me personally, I just clicked with everyone there. And I got the opportunity to conduct some real quantitative analysis. I learned a lot about writing about the developmental sector and a lot about sampling in difficult to sample areas/countries.

> Bella Vartanyan, Integrity Research Q-Step Summer Placement 2014 Student

> I feel I'm more employable. I am now looking for a new placement and in one of my interviews I talked about the Q-Step placement and they were really impressed that I have the quantitative skills and I can do data analysis. It's really helpful.
>
> Michelle Lu, Natsal (The National Survey of Sexual Attitudes and Lifestyles) at University College London, Q-Step Summer Placement 2014 Student

So far the focus has been on faculty and students. The learning is delivered by academics and teachers to students in a number of ways; through lectures, in practical lab sessions and via discussion in seminars and tutorials. The practical application of data analysis is enhanced through the work placements. What bearing then, does this have on libraries and the development of data services?

The chapters in this section will describe approaches to developing these services. In introducing this section I hope it has been evident that the prevalence of data in an undergraduate degree programme is necessitating more attention to be given to skills training to equip students in getting ready for the future world of work. Information professionals can provide much needed and valuable support in this area. How this happens through data services will vary, naturally, from country to country. The UK context, with its national provision of socioeconomic data services and teaching resources services, is well positioned to influence how local university services are established. The culture of sharing resources and good practice will help benefit all those working in this space.

This section sets out why the rise of research data services in universities is critical to supporting the current provision of student skills that will help develop them as data-literate citizens. Being part of this shared endeavour is a hugely rewarding activity; evidencing the benefits of these services to our students (incoming, present and alumni), faculty, and future employers is the next stage in this quest. The chapters presented here articulate how three institutions are making progress. We hope you will find succour in these case studies.

References

Bolton, P. (2015) *Student Loan Statistics,* House of Commons Library, http://researchbriefings.parliament.uk/ResearchBriefing/Summary/SN01079.

Buckley, J., Brown, M., Thomson, S., Olsen, W. and Carter, J. (2015) Embedding Quantitative Skills into the Social Science Curriculum: case studies from Manchester, *International Journal of Social Research Methodology,* DOI: http://

dx.doi.org/10.1080/13645579.2015.1062624.

Corti, L., Van der Eynden, V., Bishop, L. and Wollard, M. (2014) *Managing and Sharing Research Data: a guide to good practice,* London, UK, SAGE Publications Ltd.

Digital Curation Centre (2004–15) *Developing RDM Services,* Jisc, www.dcc.ac.uk/resources/developing-rdm-services.

Economic and Social Research Council (2012) *New National Digital Repository for Social and Economic Data,* www.manchester.ac.uk/discover/news/article/?id=8546.

Grundy, E. (2014) Book review of *Managing and Sharing Research Data: a guide to good practice* by Louise Corti et al., *LSE Review of Books,* http://blogs.lse.ac.uk/lsereviewofbooks/2014/08/19/book-review-managing-and-sharing-research-data-a-guide-to-good-practice.

Jisc (n.d.) *Jorum,* www.jorum.ac.uk.

Jisc (2015) *Research Data Management,* http://researchdata.jiscinvolve.org/wp.

Manyika, J., Chui, M., Brown, B., Bughin, J., Dobbs, R., Roxburgh, C. and Byers, A. H. (2011) *Big Data: the next frontier for innovation, competition, and productivity,* McKinsey Global Institute, www.mckinsey.com/insights/business_technology/big_data_the_next_frontier_for_innovation.

Nuffield Foundation (2015) *Q-Step,* www.nuffieldfoundation.org/q-step.

School of Social Sciences (n.d.) *School of Social Sciences YouTube Channel,* University of Manchester, www.youtube.com/channel/UCPwm1tKhKq7O20LoW6vEOig.

School of Social Sciences (2015) *About The University of Manchester's Q-Step Programme,* University of Manchester, https://t.co/j5llg2Ub4Y.

UC Berkeley School of Information (2015) *What is Data Science?,* http://datascience.berkeley.edu/about/what-is-data-science.

CHAPTER 4

Training researchers to manage data for better results, re-use and long-term access

Heather Coates

Introduction

The existing academic research workforce is ill-equipped to manage research data using the increasingly complex computing technologies available to them. Despite the availability of ever more powerful desktops and mobile technologies, and of high-performance cloud computing and storage, universities are failing to provide graduate students with adequate data management skills for research in academia or industry. The challenge for mid- and late-career faculty is even greater, because of the difficulty in changing established research practices for ongoing studies. This skills gap places at risk billions of research dollars, the integrity of vast quantities of research data, and the quality of life for millions of people.

Providing this workforce with the skills they need to collect, manage and share their data effectively is a challenge many academic libraries are taking on. Though libraries may provide some technological solutions, our most valuable contributions lie in expertise and trust. We have the resources to fill this skills gap by using our information management expertise, teaching ability, ability to facilitate conversation across departmental and disciplinary boundaries, and a uniquely holistic understanding of the scholarly record. At Indiana University Purdue University Indianapolis (IUPUI), education and advocacy is the foundation of our data services. This choice is shaped by the recognition that many graduate programmes are not sufficiently preparing students to manage digital research data. Before we can expect academic researchers to share, preserve and curate their data, they must understand the value and importance of data management.

This chapter will describe IUPUI's initial foray into data information literacy instruction, and the lessons learned, and look forward to the future of such programmes. We drew upon best practices in instructional design and information literacy, the scientific lab experience (Coates, 2014), and interdisciplinary data management expertise to develop the programme. The focus is on practical techniques for responsible data management and relies heavily on the data management plan (DMP) as a tool for teaching and research. Our initial trainings have reached a diverse audience, many of whom were not identified as stakeholders when developing the curriculum. This chapter will describe the development of our instructional programme, assessment results, and modifications to portray an emerging data literacy programme at a high-research-activity university.

As data has become increasingly important in academic research, confusion over terminology abounds. Bringing together researchers from diverse environments introduces uncertainty when similar terms encode different meanings for different communities. The community of library data specialists includes professionals with diverse backgrounds, and so it is useful to clarify the terms we use to discuss data skills. I use data literacy to encapsulate the skills related to finding, collecting, managing, processing, analysing, visualizing, disseminating and re-using data within the context of a research project. Data information literacy describes the skills needed for data creators, data managers and data consumers to do their work. This could include activities that take place outside the research process. When I teach, I present these skills as research data management skills. Lisa Johnston, Research Data Management/Curation Lead and Co-Director of the University Digital Conservancy at the University of Minnesota articulates this distinction very well:

> For me, data management (or RDM if you prefer) is a set of skills or best practices that can be discussed, taught, and put into practice. Other examples might be digital preservation or data visualization. These (and others) are key competencies that can be included in the overarching concept of data information literacy. But I don't tell the students that. Data information literacy is simply the binding concept that brings all of these skills and ideas into one frame of reference that I can use to define my own research in this area.
>
> Personal communication, 31 March 2015

Research is a process of discovery demanding motivation, perseverance and the ability to learn independently. Being an effective researcher requires a strong foundation of disciplinary knowledge, as well as intellectual curiosity, intrinsic motivation and metacognitive skills needed to cope with frequent obstacles encountered in the discovery process. The core of our data literacy programme includes teaching strategies for managing information and metacognitive skills that enable researchers to overcome difficulties, course correct, and ultimately persevere in the face of repeated failures. Much traditional library expertise can be translated and applied to research data management, given some knowledge and experience of the research process (Lyon, 2012; Pryor and Donnelly, 2009; Swan and Brown, 2008; Tenopir, Birch and Allard, 2012).

An informal environmental scan of our campus conducted in 2012 revealed that very few programmes offered courses in managing research data. The few that existed were very discipline-specific. Although our first step in providing data services was offering support for faculty developing NSF data management plans, conversations during workshops and consultations reinforced the need for training in digital data management. And while faculty are often targeted as high-impact stakeholders, the potential impact of training early-career researchers in more effective data management practices is higher over the long term. These practices are typically passed down from advisor to mentee and staff. Unfortunately, they are often idiosyncratic and based on outdated technologies available during the mentor's training. The significant role of mentorship in graduate training can result in passing on outmoded research practices that compromise data integrity and reproducibility. Our programme was designed to teach generalizable strategies for data management throughout the lifecycle that can be applied to current and future research technologies.

Data management lab
Background

This programme began as an informal lab pilot, but has since taken the form of a workshop series, standalone workshops and tutorials. The scope and format were informed by a scan of available courses on campus, discussions with graduate programme directors, and a review of data management curricula available at the time (DataOne, 2012; EDINA and University of Edinburgh Data Library, 2014; Cox and Verbaan, 2013). Throughout the design process, input from the Data Management group at the Indiana Clinical and Translational Sciences Institute (CTSI) provided useful guidance and targets. Tolerance for innovation within IUPUI University Library is high; we are encouraged to experiment with new services. Thus, this programme began as a grassroots effort.

While the Center for Digital Scholarship was recently established (2014), our staff have been creating digital collections of cultural heritage materials, electronic theses and dissertations, and open journals for nearly 15 years. Over the past four years, three librarians were added to expand open access initiatives and to develop support for research data and digital humanities. Current staff members include an Associate Dean of Digital Scholarship, five librarians, three full-time staff and several part-time student employees. These services and systems are supported by an internal IT team (6 FTE), who also provide support for the library website, archives, and special instructional initiatives not maintained by other institutional or campus services.

The Data Services Program, established in 2012, has been shaped strongly by the context and strategic priorities of University Library, the campus and the institution. The library's Strategic Directions include two items relevant to data: enhance the ability of IUPUI students and faculty to make their scholarly output widely accessible, and ensure its preservation (Lewis, 2015). The IUPUI Strategic Plan for Research (Indiana University – Purdue University Indianapolis, 2014) incorporates several priorities suggested by University Library: encourage wider access to findings and applications from research at IUPUI. More specific action items include the following:

> 5.2.Facilitate and increase dissemination of research and scholarship;
> 5.3.Support new metrics to assess research impact at all levels;
> 5.4.Facilitate data management re-use and archiving.
> > Indiana University – Purdue University Indianapolis, 2014

These statements emphasize data as a valid scholarly output and highlight the parallels between public access to publications and data-sharing issues. Within this context, data management is viewed as a cluster of skills crucial for the production of high-quality data, the responsible conduct of research, and long-term access to the products of academic research. The Center's mission supports the dissemination, re-use and evaluation of data as a valuable scholarly product alongside our support for publications.

Approach and audience

The ultimate goal of this programme is to provide researchers with the skills to manage their data responsibly to produce better results. Five broad priorities were identified:

1 Building awareness of research data management issues
2 Introducing methods to facilitate data integrity and address common data management issues
3 Introducing institutional resources supporting effective data management
4 Building strategic skills that enable researchers to solve new data management problems
5 Building proficiency in applying these data management methods.

These priorities emphasize the importance of data management within the research process and its role in the integrity of the scholarly record. Framing the content in this way demonstrates the relevance of data management strategies to the products of their research, which is an important motivational tool for encouraging researchers to implement these strategies.

The programme was designed to be learner-centred by using outcome-based planning and incorporating active learning strategies. Initially, the intended audiences were faculty, graduate students, and research staff. Unexpectedly, several staff from administrative units such as the Office of Research Compliance (ORC) and clinical production labs like the Indiana University Vector Performance Facility attended the fall 2014 workshops. This connection with the ORC has led to the creation of a working group established to develop institution-wide guidelines for research data management that will inform policy development and adoption.

Structure and content

Content for the data management lab was gathered from literature spanning multiple disciplines. Selected resources ranged from practice manuals such as *Good Clinical Data Management Practices* (Society for Clinical Data Management, 2013) to data-processing texts such as *Best Practices in Data Cleaning* (Osborne, 2013) to guidelines from the Office of Research Integrity (Steneck, 2004), as well as articles from computer science, library and information science, ecology and statistics. Other key resources included reports from the National Academy of Sciences (Committee on Science, Engineering and Public Policy, 2009), the UK Data Archive *Guide to Managing and Sharing Data* (Corti et al., 2014) and the ICPSR *Guide to Social Science Data Preparation and Archiving* (ICPSR, 2012). It took nearly a year to conduct the literature review and develop the curriculum and instructional plan.

Identified strategies were reviewed for curriculum inclusion based on feasibility, value and relevance to as many research methods and contexts as possible. The tentative curriculum was compared to curricula available at the time, such as Research Data MANTRA, RDMRose, and the DataONE Educational Modules. This comparison was helpful for identifying gaps in the evidence base as well as the curriculum and in balancing the needs of diverse research methods and tools. Unsurprisingly, the curriculum developed for IUPUI is very similar to those developed by other academic libraries (Coates, Muilenburg and Whitmire, 2015; Johnston and Jeffryes, 2014; Kafel, Creamer and Martin, 2014). This convergence reflects significant consensus across the community about the data management skills researchers need to succeed.

The assembled practices and strategies were organized around the DataONE data lifecycle to relate them to the research process as experienced by study personnel. This approach was selected to reflect the needs and expertise of researchers who are engaged in ongoing studies. The programme includes a broad introduction to the research data management and scholarly communication issues with the recognition that people learn what they regard as relevant. This introduction explicitly describes the connections between data literacy skills and the quality of research products, their professional reputation and the importance of quality evidence for scientific progress.

Key programme take-aways emphasize the importance of thorough planning before embarking upon data collection. Specific planning events should include (Society for Clinical Data Management, 2013):

- defining expected outcomes and quality standards for generated data
- identifying legal and ethical obligations as they affect data management, protection, security and ensuring confidentiality/privacy
- selection of tools, formats and standards
- a sound storage and back-up plan, including the use of data locks or master files
- developing an index of project and data documentation to support efficient and accurate reporting
- identifying relevant best practices for data collection, entry and coding
- identifying key expertise needed at the institutional and research community levels for informed decision-making.

These considerations and decisions are documented in the data management plan and updated as the project progresses.

Evidence-based instructional design

The format of data management and literacy training has typically consisted of one-shot workshops and standalone courses. At IUPUI, we are currently limited to providing non-credit-bearing workshops. In order to move quickly into the gap in data management education, we chose to start by offering a variety of workshops, both standalone and series. The January 2014 pilot was offered as a one-day, eight-hour workshop. Since then, the programme format varies depending on the specific audience and content that is targeted each semester. In the spring of 2014, it was offered as a four-week workshop series of weekly two-hour workshops. We scheduled evening sessions because our target audience, graduate students in the health and social sciences, often work. This proved to be less popular than expected, so subsequent events have been scheduled earlier in the day. Three key topics from the curriculum were selected for the fall 2014 line-up. Standalone workshops were offered on three topics: practical data management planning, preventing data loss and ensuring data quality. Other formats for the curriculum are planned. First, activities that are relatively straightforward and procedural will be adapted into tutorials and flipped classroom sessions. Additionally, we are exploring the feasibility of offering a for-credit course as well as embedded instruction tailored to the needs of particular departments or research centres. A long-term goal for the programme is to offer tiered and progressive instruction across the curriculum, similar to integrated information literacy programmes.

Learning outcomes for each topic were developed from best practices and recommended strategies when available. While there are gaps in the literature, the challenge in this phase was to prioritize the long list of learning outcomes into a cohesive and feasible programme. Once a reasonable list was developed, the next steps were to identify instructional design and assessment strategies. The guiding approach for this phase was to minimize lecture as much as possible in order to provide sufficient time for application through active learning exercises. This was a fairly complex process, so structure was imposed through the use of an instructional design spreadsheet (see Table 4.1). The primary form tracked modules, topics, learning outcomes, activities, assessment products, and use of case studies and examples. More specific sheets contained details about

Table 4.1 *A subset of the instructional planning spreadsheet developed for the IUPUI Data Services Program*

Module	Topic	Learning outcomes
Documentation & Metadata	Project & data documentation	Outline planned project and data documentation in a data management plan
		Identify metadata to describe the data set
		Explain the role of metadata and standards
	Organizing data & files	Develop a consistent and coherent file organization and naming convention scheme for all project files
		Select appropriate non-proprietary hardware and software formats for storing data
		Create protected copies of files at crucial points in your study
		Use versioning software or documentation for tracking changes to files over time
Data Quality	Quality assurance & control	Develop procedures for quality assurance and quality control activities
	Data collection	Describe key considerations for selecting data collection tools
	Data coding	Use best practices for coding
	Data entry	Use best practices for data entry
	Data screening & cleaning	Develop a screening and cleaning protocol and/or checklist
	Automating tasks for better provenance	Explain why automation provides better provenance than manual processes
		Identify effective tools for automating data processing and analysis

instructional timelines, assessment, and instructional materials.

We used outcome-based planning to create a learner-centred classroom that engages students with active learning techniques. In selecting recommended instructional design strategies (Clark, 2010; Nilson, 2003), four areas of focus emerged: lecture, discussion, examples and exercises. Keeping these in mind, specific activities were created to address motivation, procedural skills, strategic skills and metacognitive skills. Strategic and metacognitive skills in particular are crucial for researchers to be successful in the uncertain world of research. But teaching these skills will be ineffective if students are not motivated to learn the material. We can help motivate them by making the material relevant to their day-to-day experiences, future careers or real-world problems. The primary method we used was explaining the connection between learning outcomes to the ultimate goal of ensuring research integrity. Similar to information literacy instructional programmes, our data literacy curriculum attempts to develop strategic skills for solving new data management challenges and enable researchers to become self-regulated and self-directed learners.

Lecture

Used appropriately, lecture is a valuable component of almost any instructional programme. However, the weight of evidence for recall and application favours active learning strategies such as those that are inquiry-guided, problem-focused and collaborative (Nilson, 2003). Since it was not possible to eliminate lecture completely, the amount of time spent on lecture was minimized by focusing only on content that was strictly necessary. In general, this was realized by following established best practices based in neuropsychology. Each lecture component was brief, limited to 20 minutes (Nilson, 2003). This ensured that content was kept concise, focused only on the information needed to accomplish the learning outcomes (Clark, 2010). Each lecture began with a statement of learning outcomes and ended with a review to reinforce the connection between the content and how attendees could implement it. Presentation slides utilized a combination of text and graphics and incorporated examples whenever possible (Clark, 2010).

Discussion

Discussion, the second core component of the instructional plan, is most effective when it is activity-based, encourages reflection, and provides for formative assessment. It provides an opportunity for learners to practise self-regulation of their learning through application of metacognitive strategies. Nilson (2003) clarifies situations in which discussion is particularly effective. Those relevant to data literacy instruction include examining and changing attitudes, beliefs, values and behaviours; problem-solving; exploring unfamiliar ideas open-mindedly; and transferring knowledge to new situations. Discussion often requires more up-front planning than expected. Students need to be primed for discussion. One goal is to have them engage with each other, rather than talking through the instructor (Nilson, 2003). Specific strategies to facilitate productive discussion include waiting for responses, starting with a common experience, brainstorming what students already know about a topic, using good questioning techniques and concluding with a wrap-up (Nilson, 2003). The wrap-up ensures some closure and provides a summary; it is most effective when led by students (Nilson, 2003). We used discussions to share diverse perspectives and research experiences, build rapport and community and address complex topics such as ethical and legal obligations and choosing what data to retain for preservation.

Examples

Examples were used to make lectures and exercises more engaging and to provide concrete examples of how broad data management concepts are applied across disciplinary boundaries. Effective examples enable learners to integrate new information into a coherent structure, such as their mental model. They are especially effective when worked and partially worked examples are provided and discussed (Clark, 2010). These can facilitate procedural learning by modelling the process, which provides support for learners through each step (Clark, 2010). This can present challenges for a mixed audience of novice and experienced researchers, and so it is important to remember that while novices learn better with examples, experts do not. They benefit more greatly from time to practise (Clark, 2010). Our programme embedded examples into the lecture content and used them to support the exercises, described next.

Exercises

People learn through elaborative rehearsal and by connecting new knowledge to what they already know and believe (Nilson, 2003). In the classroom setting, exercises provide opportunities for this rehearsal. We designed exercises to be relevant, meaningful, contextualized and targeted to a particular skill. Each activity provided an opportunity to practise the strategies introduced during the lecture. Activities in the spring workshops were designed with the graduate student thesis or dissertation project in mind, to make them meaningful and contextualized. This approach met the need to provide exercises requiring application rather than recall (Clark,

2010). One effective practice we were unable to implement is distributed practice of skills over time to promote retention (Clark, 2010). Including exercises that meet all of these criteria is challenging, but implementation has improved with each iteration of the programme. Specific improvements will be discussed later, along with challenges and next steps.

The data management plan

The content and meaning of a data management plan (DMP) varies widely. For funding agencies, a DMP serves as a data collection tool to identify common practices. Researchers use the DMP as a planning tool, a part of the project start-up process, a communication mechanism throughout the project, and a resource for writing results. It is effective for both planning and implementation. However, a DMP is just one piece of good study documentation. Data management plans are functional, living documents that reflect both planning and study conduct, encompassing information that can be used in articles, reports and subsequent proposals. A DMP should reference existing standards and norms for the field. Several professional and research communities have established standards for data management and interoperability (CDISC, 2010; CDISC, 2013; Federal Geographic Data Committee, 1998; Knowledge Network for Biocomplexity, 2011). One such group is the Society for Clinical Data Management, which produces a guide to *Good Clinical Data Management Practice* (2013) that is updated biannually. It is both comprehensive and focused, covering all aspects of project management for clinical research.

The DMP is extremely valuable in the instructional context. It is a real-world product that enables authentic assessment of learning outcomes; it is an effective instructional tool because it relies on strategic skills (i.e., performance of tasks that are not routine and require problem-solving to adapt to the unique circumstances of the situation). The DMP provides an excellent opportunity for engaging learners with relevant examples and exercises. The challenges lie in developing rich cases or scenarios from which detailed DMPs can be developed if learners are not at a point in their own research to develop one. These characteristics make the DMP a uniquely powerful activity and product for assessment.

Its value as an actionable document for planning, start-up, active project phases and project completion make it worth the time needed to explain how a DMP can be used. A functional plan articulates outcomes that can be measured to identify successes and failures; it also helps researchers to anticipate problems and prevent them, gathers information needed for team communication and reporting, and enables extension, secondary use or re-use, and reproducibility of results. Perhaps most importantly, the planning process helps researchers to clearly link data quality standards to study processes, thereby producing higher quality research outputs. This is perhaps most clear in the highly regulated clinical research environment. Although the current emphasis is on its use in planning, an effective DMP, like all study documentation, should be viewed as a living document that is used frequently and updated periodically (Society for Clinical Data Management, 2013).

Strengths

Overall, evaluations for both the pilot and spring workshop series were positive. Responses to the examples were strongly positive, in session and in the evaluations. Time for discussion was appreciated and many asked for more time to continue them. Learners also appreciated the resources provided, particularly institutional services and resources, and links to further information. When asked what topics were most valuable, responses varied. Topics identified include data management plans and planning, file organization and naming, storage and back-up, master files and versioning, documentation and data citation. The evaluations also provided constructive criticism that was used to improve later offerings. During the pilot, even the experienced staff stated that a full eight-hour day was too much; they felt overwhelmed. In the spring, content was separated into four workshops of two hours each. This format provided sufficient time to engage students with exercises, while alleviating the weight of providing all the content at once. It also provided students time to reflect between sessions, which enhanced discussion because they were better able to make connections between the topics.

Challenges and next steps

Although the evaluations spoke to the relevance and utility of the programme to their research, there remains substantial room for improvement. In particular, there is much to be done to optimize instructional design and delivery and expand its reach to the research community at IUPUI. Possibly the most significant challenge was not knowing where students are starting from (Nilson, 2003). Within the graduate student population alone, there is a wide range of experience with research. Some are professionals seeking education to advance or change careers, while others have just finished their undergraduate work. Teaching researchers with such a diverse range of experience is difficult; some strategies are more effective for novices than experts, and vice versa, making it difficult to develop learning outcomes, choose exercises and select relevant examples. One option is incorporating topic-specific pre-assessments into the beginning of each session to prime learners and target instruction more effectively. Another is to have learners complete a broad pre-assessment prior to the programme. Unfortunately, no such assessment currently exists.

Despite positive evaluations, attrition was high throughout the spring series of workshops. While 23 attendees registered, only slightly more than half (12) attended the first session. By the fourth and final session, just four students remained. It may be possible to improve this with better timing, but retention is generally a problem for non-credit bearing workshops on our campus. We are exploring other incentives to promote retention, as well as the possibility for partnering with an academic department to provide a for-credit graduate course.

The third significant adjustment is to provide better support for relating data management skills to existing knowledge and experiences. As Nilson (2003) reminds us, we need to teach students how to learn the material. We hope to accomplish this by explicitly connecting individual learning outcomes with the broader goals and skills they will gain. For each session, we will provide an empty outline of the key points for students to fill in along with a background knowledge probe. We will facilitate attendees relating new ideas to their existing knowledge by providing time for reflection and explicitly discussing the connections between the learning outcomes and the students' area of research. Tools like concept maps are time-consuming to use, but the burden on the instructor could be alleviated by using peer review to provide helpful feedback.

There are many minor adjustments to be made. We have already begun to try workshops that cover fewer topics in order to delve more deeply and provide more opportunities for application. While the design for the spring workshop series attempted to build in plenty of assessment opportunities (Nilson, 2003), execution in the classroom was less than ideal. We will further examine the activities and assessment products to ensure we provide adequate motivation and clearly state the connection to learning outcomes. Specifically, formative assessment of data management plans and documentation will be incorporated primarily through peer review (Whitmire, 2014). Ideally, summative assessment will be added to gather evidence of behaviour change and implementation of learned strategies. We will build in additional time to complete the formative assessments, review them and respond to them. There are also plans to teach more explicitly the metacognitive skills to promote self-regulation of learning within their own research.

Future of data literacy instruction
Opportunities

We face several important questions as the demand for these skills within and outside the academy increases. When do we provide data literacy instruction? When is it most relevant and useful for students? Information literacy research has found that support and instruction are most powerful at the point of need, but there are many such points that arise throughout the research process. How do we reach students during those times? And how do we help students identify when they need support? Further research into these questions is necessary for instruction to proceed beyond a trial and error approach to meeting the needs of our researchers.

I see two immediate opportunities. If we want to better adapt data literacy instruction to students, we need to develop pre-assessments that accurately gauge their knowledge of disciplinary research practices as well as the research process. The most pressing needs for data literacy instruction are authentic, engaging examples and activities. While many participants have pre-existing projects, students who are novice researchers need the support of relevant examples and well structured exercises. Such resources rely on real-world datasets that are curated for instruction purposes, rather than for re-use. Developing scenarios and case studies are time-consuming and can be difficult to tailor to specific fields of research if the instructor is unfamiliar with them. Just as librarians have developed rich resources for information literacy instruction, we need a repository for instructional materials, cases and scenarios to effectively teach data literacy. This should include activities and assignments relevant to disciplinary practices and which provide opportunities for authentic assessment. The data management plan is just one of these activities. Second, we need to identify foundational data management skills and determine the optimal sequence of learning outcomes that enable students to practise responsible data management within their own discipline. This will require the data librarian and specialist community to leverage the expertise of our instructional and liaison colleagues.

Moving forward, the community of instructors teaching data literacy, including faculty and librarians, has several issues to address in order to develop sustainable models for instruction. We should explicitly acknowledge the many roles through which people interact with research data – creator, manager and consumer. In these early days, we can simply build in support for data literacy alongside existing information literacy services such as reference and instruction, content guides, citation tools and training, first-year experience programmes and discipline-based programmes. Rather than creating new models for service, it may be more sustainable to train library staff to deliver data content and instruction in the context of their daily work. For those data specialists or managers tasked with developing or co-ordinating support for researchers, this could take several forms (Tenopir et al., 2013). However, models which simply extend existing services (such as reference, instruction and liaison activities) to include data are less well documented.

The future of data literacy instruction at IUPUI

The future of our programme will include broadening the range of formats by offering targeted materials and activities for use by faculty in discipline-specific courses, a for-credit graduate course, self-paced tutorials, as well as general workshops and on-demand instructional sessions. In particular, we need to develop mechanisms to deliver point-of-need support alongside embedded support within particular academic courses. Of course, the ultimate goal for data literacy instruction is to demonstrate long-term impact and application of these skills in the research happening on our campuses. For that, we can look to the literature on demonstrating the value of academic library for examples and strategies. People learn when they are motivated to do so by the inspiration and enthusiasm of others (Nilson, 2003). Instructors can tap into their own passion and energy by finding the aspects of data literacy that are compelling to them, and can in turn help students connect with their interests by sharing stories of failure and success.

References

Clark, R. C. (2010) *Evidence-based Training Methods: a guide for training professionals*, Alexandria, VA, ASTD Press.

Clinical Data Interchange Standards Consortium (CDISC) (2010) *Clinical Data Acquisition Standards Harmonization* (CDASH, v. 1.1).

Clinical Data Interchange Standards Consortium (CDISC) (2013) *Study Data Tabulation Model* (v. 1.4), CDISC Submission Data Standards Team.

Coates, H. L. (2014) *Teaching Data Literacy Skills in a Lab Environment*, paper presented to the International Association for Social Science Information Services and Technology, Toronto, Canada, http://hdl.handle.net/1805/4538.

Coates, H. L., Muilenburg, J. and Whitmire, A. L. (2015) *Promoting Sustainable Research Practices Through Effective Data Management Curricula*, paper presented to the Association of College and Research Libraries, Portland, OR, http://hdl.handle.net/1805/6043.

Committee on Science, Engineering and Public Policy (2009) *On Being a Scientist: a guide to responsible conduct in research*, Washington, DC, The National Academies Press.

Corti, L., Van den Eynden, V., Bishop, L. and Woollard, M. (2014) *Managing and Sharing Research Data: a guide to good practice*, London, UK, SAGE Publications Ltd.

Cox, A. and Verbaan, E. (2013) *RDMRose Learning Materials*, www.sheffield.ac.uk/is/research/projects/rdmrose.

DataOne (2012) *Education Modules for Data Management*, www.dataone.org/education-modules.

EDINA and University of Edinburgh Data Library (2014) *Research Data MANTRA*, online course, http://datalib.edina.ac.uk/mantra.

Federal Geographic Data Committee (1998) *Content Standard for Digital Geospatial Metadata.*

ICPSR (Inter-university Consortium for Political and Social Research) (2012) *Guide to Social Science Data Preparation and Archiving: best practice throughout the data life cycle*, Ann Arbor, MI, www.icpsr.umich.edu/files/ICPSR/access/dataprep.pdf.

Indiana University – Purdue University Indianapolis (IUPUI) (2014) *Research Strategic Plan, Indiana University – Purdue University Indianapolis*, http://research.iupui.edu/stratinit/documents/researchstrategicplan101414.pdf.

Johnston, L. and Jeffryes, J. (2014) Steal This Idea: a library instructors' guide to educating students in data management skills, *College & Research Libraries News*, **75** (8), 431–4.

Kafel, D., Creamer, A. and Martin, E. (2014) Building the New England Collaborative Data Management Curriculum, *Journal of eScience Librarianship*, **3** (1), 60–6, DOI: 10.7191/jeslib.2014.1066.

Knowledge Network for Biocomplexity (2011) *Ecological Metadata Language* (v. 2.1.1).

Lewis, D. (2015) *University Library Strategic Directions*, Indiana University – Purdue University Indianapolis.

Lyon, L. (2012) The Informatics Transform: re-engineering libraries for the data decade, *International Journal of Digital Curation*, **7** (1), 126–38, DOI: 10.2218/ijdc.v7i1.220.

Nilson, L. B. (2003) *Teaching at its Best: a research-based resource for college instructors*, Bolton, MA, Anker Publishing Co.

Osborne, J. W. (2013) *Best Practices in Data Cleaning: a complete guide to everything you need to do before and after collecting your data*, Thousand Oaks, CA, SAGE.

Pryor, G. and Donnelly, M. (2009) Skilling Up to do Data: whose role, whose responsibility, whose career?, *International Journal of Digital Curation*, **4** (2), 158–70.

Society for Clinical Data Management (2013) *Good Clinical Data Management Practices*, Brussels, Belgium.

Steneck, N. H. (2004) *ORI Introduction to the Responsible Conduct of Research*, Washington, DC, Government Printing Office.

Swan, A. and Brown, S. (2008) *The Skills, Role and Career Structure of Data Scientists and Curators: an assessment of current practice and future needs*, London, UK, Jisc, www.jisc.ac.uk/media/documents/programmes/digitalrepositories/dataskillscareersfinalreport.pdf.

Tenopir, C., Birch, B. and Allard, S. (2012) *Academic Libraries and Research Data Services: current practices and plans for the future; an ACRL White Paper*, Association of College and Research Libraries, www.ala.org/acrl/sites/ala.org.acrl/files/content/publications/whitepapers/Tenopir_Birch_Allard.pdf.

Tenopir, C., Sandusky, R., Allard, S. and Birch, B. (2013) Academic Librarians and Research Data Services: preparation and attitudes, *IFLA Journal*, **39**, 70–8, DOI: 10.1177/0340035212473089.

Whitmire, A. (2014) *Implementing a Graduate-level Data Information Literacy Curriculum at Oregon State University: approach, outcomes and lessons learned,* poster presented at the University of Massachusetts and New England Area Librarian e-Science Symposium, Worcester, MA, http://ir.library.oregonstate.edu/xmlui/handle/1957/47005.

CHAPTER 5

Data services for the research lifecycle: the Digital Social Science Center

Ashley Jester

Introduction: supporting data in the libraries

While data has been a feature of academic research since the early 20th century, it is only in the last decade that it has become such a ubiquitous feature of academic life – and all modern experience – that it has taken root in all aspects of the education environment. Concomitant with the rise in the awareness of 'data' as both a concept for debate and discussion and an object of study and analysis has been the rise of the idea of 'data literacy' or the ability to understand and interpret data. Different institutions have responded to the growth of data differently, and these choices often reflect circumstances of time as much as institutional traditions and organizational structures. This chapter will discuss how support for data has developed and grown at Columbia University Libraries, specifically within the Digital Social Science Center (herein, DSSC). While much of the development of data services at Columbia can be traced to a specific set of circumstances existing at a particular point in time, the overall trajectory of these services presents several general principles that can provide insights for other institutions.

Defining data literacy

Before delving into the specifics of data services at Columbia, it is worthwhile to discuss some of the basic elements of data literacy. At its most basic level, being data-literate means that someone understands what data is and how data can be used. Data as a concept is rather broad, and I would argue that nearly anything could be considered data in certain circumstances. In the simplest terms, data is information that has defined parameters that give it some sense of structure. The degree of structure varies widely, and many people are likely familiar with data sources that produce rather 'dirty' results, such as data that is scraped from government agencies' websites or extracted from a Twitter feed. Nevertheless, even 'messy' or 'dirty' data has a fundamental element of structure in the sense that there are parameters defining the information contained in the dataset. These parameters include the unit of observation (i.e., the individual elements that make up the collected data), the variables/measures (i.e., the information that is recorded about each unit of observation), and the time period in which the observations were collected and/or created. Different datasets have differing degrees of structure in these parameters, and this is not intended to be an exhaustive list. Rather, the point I wish to emphasize here is that data is a broad concept that encompasses gathered information of many forms – numbers, descriptive categories, text, images, and audio and video clips can all be data.

Just as data can take on different forms, it can also have many different uses. Data can be used to present an historical narrative of a situation in which the data is used to construct a picture or model of a particular point in time. Consider the use of historic trade data: by analysing and reporting information about commodity flows from various ports around the world in the 1900s, someone can construct a model of what trade looked like during this period. Data can also be used to make predictions about future behaviour or outcomes. For example, data about the current financial situations of various companies is used to make predictions about what those companies' financial health will look like in the coming months and years. The financial/banking research industry is predicated on the idea that data such as this can be leveraged for predictive power. Data can also be used to test hypotheses and theories. In the social sciences and humanities, where laboratory experiments are rare, the use of observational data to test hypotheses derived from theoretical frameworks is a key element in the advancement of knowledge.

Data literacy can be considered the combination of two areas of understanding – knowing what data *is* and understanding how data is used. There is not a single on/off switch that indicates that one has achieved 'data literacy.' Rather, it should be considered a spectrum of skills and knowledge. One of the goals of the data services we provide at Columbia is to support and enhance the data literacy of our users. Our staff is keenly aware of the need to engage with all users as researchers, and in our research consultations we strive to emphasize a firm understanding of the data itself and how it can be used appropriately to meet the desired ends of the user. Promoting data literacy is the foundation of all the data services provided at the DSSC.

Creating data services at Columbia

The term 'data services' encompasses a broad swathe of activities in academic libraries, and it seems that nearly every institution has its own definition. For us at the DSSC, data services are the suite of research support services that relate directly to the discovery and use of data. This includes identification and discovery of data sources. Data services also include support for cleaning and formatting data using a variety of software tools, both licensed and open-source. Our support includes the use of the analytical tools, both for quantitative and qualitative data, such as Stata, R, SAS and SPSS, and those used for geospatial data, like ArcGIS and QGIS. Finally, our data support extends to research methodology and data analysis, including support for geospatial and statistical analysis. Support for data visualization is included, since it can be thought of as another form of data analysis and interpretation that relies upon visual space. I like to refer to the DSSC's data services as 'nose-to-tail' research support – we provide assistance at every step of the research lifecycle, from planning a project and identifying an appropriate data source through the final publication and presentation of the results of data analysis.

Data services are a subset of the overall reference and research support offered in the DSSC, and we consider all of these services and support to be complementary to one another. In other words, while we distinguish data services as a distinct set of services aimed at supporting data for research, teaching and learning, we see these services as part of the overall research support we offer. This integration of data services with more general research support has been an evolution, but we believe that embedding data services in the larger research context, particularly by using the research lifecycle as a guide, not only enhances our overall research support but also strengthens the data services we offer. For us, a comprehensive and holistic approach to research support is part of our identity as the DSSC – we want to be a place where researchers of all types can come at any point in their project to receive support and service.

The evolution of data services at Columbia

Prior to the creation of the Electronic Data Services, a precursor to the current DSSC, the university's central information technology division handled data services at Columbia University. There has long been a need for the support of electronic data in research, stemming not only from the natural sciences and engineering fields but also from the social sciences. In fact, the social sciences are in many ways the leader in this area as the Inter-university Consortium for Political and Social Research (ICPSR) has existed for more than 50 years as a data repository (ICPSR, n.d.). Prior to 1994, Columbia's central academic computing division handled the university's membership in ICPSR and was responsible for providing data services to the Columbia community.

In 1994, two developments led to the creation of the Electronic Data Services. The first was the desire of Columbia's central academic computing group to exit its role in providing data services. Their focus was beginning to shift and no longer included offering support for access to the data housed at ICPSR. Nevertheless, there was still a need for support of ICPSR's collections. At this time, ICPSR data was still distributed via magnetic tapes, and accessing and processing the files for use in statistical analysis required programmatic expertise. Thus, any new solution would require information technology experts, though there was also recognition that subject expertise could add significant value to any services related to the ICPSR collection.

At the same time, the 1990 US Decennial Census was made available through electronic means for the first time on CD-ROMs. While it's hard to believe now, when CD-ROMs were first introduced, most researchers were completely unfamiliar with this format, and most personal computers were not equipped with CD-ROM drives. Beyond Columbia's obligation as a federal depository library to support the use of this collection, there was the significant demand from researchers within the university community for access to the Census data. Given the Census's important place in social science research, the question was not whether the university would support the use of this new technology but how this support would be provided.

Given these dual demands (access to ICPSR and access to the 1990 US Census) it was decided that Columbia University Libraries should have a support role, due to their tradition as providers of information services. While the format of the information (i.e., electronic data) was new for the Libraries, the role of providing discovery and access to information was – and remains – part of its core responsibilities. The importance of this decision for the emergence of data services in Columbia can only be appreciated in retrospect. Had circumstances been slightly different or had a different solution been selected, it is not obvious that Electronic Data Services and, eventually, the DSSC, would have been created.

The next detail to decide was where this service would be offered and how personnel would be assigned. Ultimately, Electronic Data Services was created in the Social Sciences Division as a joint project between the Libraries and central university academic computing. The initial staff included both library professionals and information technologists and programmers from academic computing. Programmers were included because in the mid-1990s, access to data from ICPSR still required direct mediation from professional staff and CD-ROMs were an emerging technology with which most researchers were unfamiliar. Library professionals were included because the discovery and utilization of this data required the support of subject experts familiar with these collections and capable of assisting researchers with identifying the data that would best suit their needs. Although the close partnership between the Libraries and central academic computing has dissipated over the years, the initial model of support for both subject and technological expertise has remained an enduring feature of the current DSSC.

The creation of Electronic Data Services provided a durable foundation upon which all of the data services at Columbia and the DSSC have been built. The development of data services at Columbia has been an evolutionary process, both in response to the needs of the university community and by Columbia taking the lead in adopting new technology and advocating its use within the research community. At various points we at the DSSC have been both responsive and generative; we have both met existing demands and created new ones through the supply of innovative services.

Data services in practice: the role of the DSSC

One consistent feature of data services at the DSSC has been a team-based approach to research support. A great strength of the DSSC, and of Columbia University Libraries overall, is the wide range of expertise found among our staff. There is a great deal of both breadth and depth in the skills of our staff members, and this means that, for practically every discipline and approach, there is someone in the Libraries who has expertise and can provide support. Given that no single staff member can be an expert on everything required to support research, we instead rely upon referrals and a collaborative working environment in which we share responsibilities for providing data services. It is not unusual for two or more staff members to work with a patron on a given project, sometimes working concurrently to solve complicated multidisciplinary problems and sometimes working consecutively as the researcher progresses through the different stages of her project. This team-based approach not only allows us to serve a wider range of research needs than any of us could support working alone but also provides for a supportive working environment for our staff members, who can be comfortable with the limits of their individual knowledge since there is always the option of making a referral or calling in a colleague for assistance. Having a strong team allows each of us to leverage both our subject and technical expertise when assisting researchers, while relying upon the comparative advantages of our colleagues to extend our support for data services beyond the limits of our own skills. What binds us together is a common commitment to providing research support that enables and enhances data literacy and promotes the development of individual users as researchers.

In the DSSC, our team has found that the research lifecycle provides a useful framework for organizing our support for data services with an eye toward data literacy. A simple four-phase model of this lifecycle helps to structure the services and support offered in the DSSC (see Figure 5.1).

All researchers, whether they are undergraduates beginning their first projects or tenured faculty working on advanced agendas, can identify with

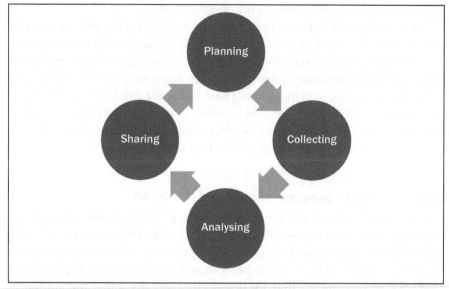

Figure 5.1 *The four-phase model of the research lifecycle*

the phases of the research lifecycle. More importantly, we as library and information professionals can use this lifecycle model to tailor our services and support to meet the needs of the researcher in the moment, utilizing an on-demand and just-in-time model. Using the reference interview as a starting point, we can discern what types of services are appropriate for this moment in the research project as well as develop a plan for providing services and support throughout the remainder of the work. Building upon this research lifecycle framework, I will discuss the ways that this model has been used to structure research support, in particular data services, at Columbia.

Planning
Most of the time, researchers arrive in the DSSC after they have already begun their research projects; thus, we are not always able to work with a researcher during this phase. Nevertheless, knowing about the work that is undertaken in the planning phase is incredibly important to our ability to provide data services to the researcher. Specifically, it is critical for us to understand what the goals of the research project are and what kind of data will be required to answer the research question or questions being posed.

In the planning phase, researchers set a research agenda, ideally one that includes details about the steps that will be undertaken during the future stages of the research lifecycle. Depending upon the particular discipline or methodological approach, this may include the development of a research question or questions. For social scientists, this typically means stating a theoretical framework and a hypothesis (or hypotheses) to be tested in the coming research project. Researchers in the humanities often do not use such formal scientific language to describe their research projects, but many still share the same elements of research design. In general, all research is aimed at uncovering new information through a careful approach to studying a particular problem or question, and it is the preparation for this study that comprises the planning phase of the research lifecycle.

Whether the researcher arrives after the planning has happened or before any preparations have begun, the staff at the DSSC use the reference interview to discover information about the approach that will be used in a given research project. Since providing useful data services requires us to understand the needs of a researcher, it is important that we prompt the researcher with questions about the question or questions she would like to answer. In addition to understanding the goals of the research project, we also want to learn about the methodological approach that will be used, since this will also influence the types and sources of data that will be recommended. With an understanding of the goals and approach of the research project, we can advise the researcher on collecting data, whether from primary or secondary sources.

Collecting

The core services that we provide in the DSSC are centred on the next two phases of the research lifecycle: collecting and analysing. In the collecting phase of the cycle, researchers are gathering the research materials they will need to answer their research questions, including the testing of hypotheses. Support for collecting data in the DSSC can be traced back to its roots as the Electronic Data Services, where the focus was on discovery and access to data. As noted in the previous section, library professionals provided support for identifying appropriate data sources, and information technologists provided support for accessing and using data. In the DSSC, these two roles have been blended into support for collecting data that is provided by all members of our team.

Collecting data comes in two basic forms – original (or primary) data collection and secondary data collection. In original data collection, researchers create new data through observation, by combing primary source materials, or running experiments (this is not an exhaustive list of the ways that primary research data are created, but rather some common examples). In secondary data collection, researchers rely upon existing data sources to gather the information they need to complete their research. Many social scientists use a mixture of both types of data collection in their research, with some data being the product of original work and other data being drawn from existing sources. At the DSSC, we assist users with both.

When the researcher is working on original data collection, the focus of the data services provided in the DSSC is on 'clean' data collection. This means working with the researcher to make sure that the data collection is done in a consistent way, with documentation that allows the researcher to review what she has done and also allows future researchers to replicate her efforts. Original data collection is closely tied to the planning phase of the research lifecycle, since it's important to have a data collection plan in place before gathering any observations.

Original data collection necessitates choosing an appropriate instrument for data collection and using it correctly. The term 'instrument' is drawn from the natural sciences where instruments are typically pieces of physical lab equipment that record measurements for experiments. In the social sciences, instruments take many forms. For some types of research, instruments are indeed pieces of physical equipment; this is especially true in fields where studies are conducted directly on human subjects or the environment, such as the fields of public health, development and archaeology. In other cases, instruments are more conceptual constructs; surveys, observational protocols or measurement scales. Regardless of the instrument's format, it is important to be sure that it has been calibrated properly and provides consistent data collection for every observation. In the DSSC, we discuss with researchers issues of instrument selection, calibration and consistency. Some example services include setting up a data collection form based on a research protocol, assisting with survey design and testing, demonstrating the use of technology used to take measurements, or discussing how to check for consistency in measurements. We are able to provide this type of assistance because of the expertise of our staff; several of our librarians hold doctorates and thus can address issues of instrumentation drawing upon their academic training and experience with advanced research methods. Other members of our staff have advanced degrees that have provided training around the use of particular sorts of instruments for social science research; again, they are able to provide guidance and assistance by drawing upon both a strong theoretical understanding and direct practical knowledge. Using our team-based approach, we can meet the diverse needs of researchers in choosing or designing their instrument and evaluating its efficacy for data collection.

Another role is helping researchers ensure that their collection methods are well documented, both for their own benefit and for the requirements of future reproducibility. While good data documentation is important for original data collection, it also critical in support of data collection involving secondary sources. Whether data is being created originally or gathered from existing sources, it is paramount that researchers document the data. Our staff assists with data documentation not only by suggesting appropriate tools for managing documentation, including citation management and electronic lab notebooks, as necessary, but also by providing guidance about the purpose and practice of data documentation. Consistent with our focus on promoting data literacy, we approach data documentation from the standpoint of the purpose it serves in the research lifecycle. Data documentation provides individual researchers with a record of how and when data was collected, what manipulations may have occurred in the collection process, and the way in which the collected data has been organized and stored for use. This same documentation also supplies the information necessary for future researchers to replicate the data collection process and independently verify the collected data or expand and extend the range of the dataset.

For researchers collecting secondary data, the process begins with understanding the goals and scope of the research project. The reference interview is a vital part of this process, as it enables us to understand the needs and expectations of the researcher. Fundamentally, in order to advise on secondary data collection, the questions of what, when and where need to be answered regarding the research project. When conducting a reference interview focused on secondary data collection, some of the key questions are:

- What is the timeline of your research project? How much time do you have to devote to gathering, processing and analysing the data you need?
- What is the time period you are studying? Do you need cross-sectional, longitudinal or panel data to answer your question?
- What is the geography associated with your project? At what level of geography do you need to collect observations to answer your research questions?
- What are the key concepts you need to measure to test your hypotheses or answer your research questions? How would you like to operationalize these concepts?

Our strategy for working with researchers collecting secondary data is to use the reference interview to evaluate not only the needs and expectations of the researcher but also her skills and understanding (i.e., her data literacy). Needs and expectations must be matched to the level of data literacy so that the secondary data sources we suggest meet the research requirements of the project and the abilities of the researcher. For example, while the Integrated Public Use Microdata Series available from the Minnesota Population Center is a rich resource that can be used in a variety of social science data projects, it requires a high level of data literacy, as researchers need to be familiar with the use of microdata and the statistical methods associated with working with these types of samples (University of Minnesota, n.d.). Our policy at the DSSC is to meet researchers where they are – we do not suggest using data sources that require advanced data literacy skills unless the researcher already has them or is willing to acquire them as part of the research project.

In some cases, the exact secondary data that a researcher is seeking does not exist. In these cases, we are able to offer two paths to a solution. The first is for the researcher to consider an original data collection project. If we are able to identify a primary source for the information she is seeking, it is possible for the researcher to collect the data herself. As with all original data collection projects, this is time-consuming but may be the best option if a good substitute cannot be found. The other path is to identify alternatives that, while not the exact data that the researcher envisioned, can be good substitutes. Finding appropriate substitutes relies upon the information gathered in the reference interview, in particular the information about what concepts need to be measured in order to test hypotheses or answer research questions. If direct measurement of a particular concept is not possible, it may be possible to find secondary data sources that capture related information that is correlated with the concept and thus works as a substitute. Similarly, some concepts (e.g., criminal activity and corruption) are notoriously difficult to find directly measured, but there may be other types of data sources that capture information about these concepts without a direct measurement. Whenever a researcher is unable to locate the exact data source she is seeking, the staff in the DSSC use the information from the reference interview to suggest an appropriate solution, whether that means collecting original data or substituting other secondary data.

Overall, the DSSC's approach centres on a firm understanding of the researcher's needs and expectations, gleaned from the reference interview, combined with a clear view of the researcher's data literacy.

Analysing

Once data has been collected, the next step in the research lifecycle is analysis. The transition between the collecting and analysing phases involves data cleaning, including manipulation and combination as necessary. Some will consider this part of the collecting phase while others may put this step in the analysing phase, but, data cleaning is an essential step in the research process. In the DSSC, we think about data cleaning as the first steps in the analysing phase – the data has been collected, but now it must be prepared for analysis. Cleaning data can range from relatively simple manipulations like recoding variables or combining datasets to more complicated processes such as transforming measures or categorizing missing and incomplete observations. As with the collecting phase, proper data documentation is a key part of this process; researchers need to make it clear what decisions they made with respect to their data and how the raw data has been transformed prior to analysis. Since DSSC staff members have specialized expertise in software packages and programming languages, we offer assistance with data cleaning using a wide variety of tools, including Excel, Stata, SPSS, R, SAS, ArcGIS, QGIS, Python and Perl.

When working with researchers, we emphasize that collecting and cleaning data take up a large part of the research project timeline. Once data is cleaned and prepared for analysis, the time required is surprisingly short, as the advances in analytical software and computational power mean that even complex operations can be performed in a matter of minutes, if not seconds. At the DSSC, we support data analysis in two dimensions. First, we provide the software and hardware necessary to perform analysis. Second, more importantly, we supply subject expertise that supports not only the use of the software and hardware but also the theoretical understanding of statistical methodology and research design.

While it is not uncommon for research libraries to support data analysis by providing hardware and software, the support for statistical methodology and research design is more rare. This support for statistical methodology and research design is a part of the data services that has emerged only in the last few years as staff members with the necessary expertise have joined the DSSC. Analytical support is one of the areas where we have seen the largest growth in demand for data services. Once we began to advertise that researchers could get assistance not only with the software and hardware used to analyse data but could also receive advice on their research design and the appropriate statistical model needed to test their hypotheses, users began to arrive in droves for these services. What we learned through this process was that there was an unmet need on campus for statistical support, one which we are able to meet. Thus, at the DSSC, we view this part of our data services as a unique contribution to the Columbia community. We are the only place at Columbia University where anyone, regardless of the department or programme in which they are enrolled, can get assistance with finding, using and analysing research data. Despite being called the Digital *Social Science* Center, we see researchers from all across the disciplinary spectrum – natural scientists and humanists are just as likely to turn up in the DSSC looking for assistance with data analysis as social scientists. With our open-door policy and walk-in hours for assistance, we have established the DSSC as a critical node for research support at Columbia University. While there are other places where researchers can get assistance with data analysis, we are the only place that is open to everyone and free to use.

The DSSC's approach to supporting data analysis is similar to our approach for data collection, relying on a reference interview to assess the needs and expectations of the researcher. Some of the questions that are important for a data analysis reference interview are:

- What is the timeline of your research project? How much time do you have to devote to analysing your data and interpreting the results?
- What does your data look like? How are the key concepts operationalized and measured? How familiar are you with the content of your data? Are there structures in your data that limit the types of analysis available to you?
- What kinds of questions do you need to answer about your data? What are the hypotheses you need to test?
- What methodological approach do you plan to use? How familiar are you with the analytical techniques of this methodology? Have you used these methods before? What tools are you planning to use for the analysis?

After assessing where the researcher stands, DSSC staff work with her to develop a plan for data analysis. Again taking the approach of meeting the researcher where she is, we suggest both analytical tools (such as software or programming languages) and methodological approaches that will meet the needs and expectations of the researcher. At the DSSC, our policy is that we do not do the work for the researcher but rather guide and teach the researcher to do the work herself. As such, while we are happy to demonstrate how to execute a particular type of analysis or discuss the theory behind a methodology, we will not advise researchers to use methods that they do not understand and cannot explain in simple language. Since all data analysis ends with interpreting the results of the analytical operations, it is essential that the researcher is able to do this interpretation on her own. While our staff have the skills and knowledge necessary to assist with interpreting the results of analysis, such assistance crosses the line from *supporting* research to *doing* research. The purpose of our data services is to offer support to researchers doing their own work, not to do the work for them.

Sharing

After data has been collected, analysed and interpreted, research results are reported. Sometimes this takes the form of written publications; in other situations, research results may be a slideshow or poster presentation. Regardless of the particular form, however, there is a finished 'product' that represents the culmination of the research process. How this product is distributed constitutes the final stage of the research lifecycle: sharing.

While this is not part of the core data services of collecting and analysing that comprise our major focus, it is part of the research lifecycle for which we are offering support. At the DSSC, we offer researchers assistance with sharing their research products, with a particular focus on sharing data. At Columbia University Libraries, we are able to partner with colleagues from the Center for Digital Research and Scholarship (CDRS), a centre that is focused on the sharing of research products. Staff from the DSSC frequently collaborate with the staff of CDRS to support researchers with digital publishing and providing open access to their research results, in particular through Columbia University's institutional repository, Academic Commons (Columbia University Libraries/Information Services, n.d.). Additionally, DSSC staff provide guidance and assistance with navigating the vast resources available outside of the Columbia community as publishing venues, including depositing data in ICPSR. Our goal is to work with the researcher to identify the best home for their research products.

Our strategy for working with researchers open to sharing their data is to emphasize that publishing research data enables researchers to receive credit from the scholarly community for their contribution. We explain the role of data citations, in addition to citations for other publications, as an important part of a researcher's overall portfolio. As part of this discussion, DSSC staff also provide information on alternative citation metrics and suggest ways that researchers can improve the visibility of their published data. The DSSC aims to help researchers see how the sharing phase of the research lifecycle fits into the overall landscape of the research process. After all, if researchers did not share their data, the supply of secondary data available for collection and analysis would not exist. While sharing is often an after-thought to researchers at the end of a long research project, we believe it is important to emphasize how sharing research products enables the entire lifecycle to begin anew.

Conclusions – data services and the research lifecycle

Through this chapter, I have discussed the ways that the staff of the DSSC at Columbia University Libraries use the research lifecycle framework to organize our data services. An essential piece of this support is the role of data literacy in underpinning our services. As I have discussed, in the DSSC we view supporting and enhancing data literacy as the foundation upon which our data services are built. In concert with this foundation, we use the research lifecycle framework to organize our support. Relying upon the information gathered through a reference interview, we are able to identify where a researcher is in the lifecycle, assess her needs and expectations, and respond with support that meets the researcher where she is.

Providing data services in the Libraries at Columbia University means that we are able to meet the demand from the entire research community, and it has lowered the barrier to entry for researchers seeking support. Since the Libraries have traditionally been the place where everyone is welcome, regardless of their discipline or programme, offering data services through this venue has resulted in a broad reach impossible to achieve in other locations. Furthermore, by joining together subject and technical expertise, it enables us to provide seamless support for all phases of the research lifecycle. Leveraging the wide range of expertise available among our staff and taking a team-based approach to data services has allowed the DSSC to grow into a one-stop shop for researchers looking for support. As we continue to grow and develop, our goal is to listen to the needs of the research community and respond to changes in the academic environment as needed. Moreover, because of our extensive experience with providing data services and research support more generally, we can help to shape the direction in which the research community at Columbia University evolves. Our continuing commitment to supporting data literacy will ensure that the future of the data services at Columbia University Libraries is one that supports the research lifecycle and enables the production of high-quality research that has impact both within the Columbia community and without the wider research world.

References

Columbia University Libraries/Information Services (n.d.) *Center for Digital Research and Scholarship*, http://cdrs.columbia.edu.

ICPSR (Inter-university Consortium for Political and Social Research) (n.d.) *ICPSR: the founding and early years*, University of Michigan, www.icpsr.umich.edu/icpsrweb/content/membership/history/early-years.html.

University of Minnesota (n.d.) *Minnesota Population Center: Integrated Public Use Microdata Series*, www.ipums.org.

CHAPTER 6

Mapping unusual research needs: supporting GIS across non-traditional disciplines

Karen Munro

What is GIS?

A regional planner is studying a map that shows the boundary of a local watershed, the location of natural gas deposits beneath the ground and the ownership of the land. But the planner knows that the watershed boundary was redrawn last spring, and that the company that owned the land has since sold it to a conservation group.

A young architect designing a new city transit centre clicks and scrolls through a digital map of Portland, OR. The map shows the city's river and bridges, streets, highways, and even the individual building outlines, kerbs and sidewalks. But it's a map of the entire city, and the architect only needs to see a few neighbourhoods. The image is high-resolution, meaning the file is huge and it takes a lot of processing power to continually load and redraw it on the screen. The architect has to scroll, pan and resize constantly to navigate. In exasperation she prints it out – and finds that it's ten feet long and four feet wide.

A journalist stares glumly at a familiar map of the USA, one which shows state and national borders as well as capital cities. She can easily see the geographic area in question – but what she really wants to know is how income levels in the northeast compare to those in the southwest. The map is useless to her, so she goes back online to find another.

In all three of these situations, the user's problems could have been resolved with geographic information systems (GIS). But although GIS has been in wide use by geographers for decades, many other professions are unaware of its potential. This is ironic, since many of us now use GIS on a regular basis, even daily, through popular and free end-user applications such as Google Maps. But GIS isn't just about finding your blue dot on the freeway exit map, or asking where the closest Starbucks is. For students conducting academic research, GIS can be a powerful tool, adding unexpected depth and power to projects across a wide range of disciplines – and librarians can help make it happen.

Most simply put, GIS is a means of making information about a place visible, flexible and reconfigurable on a map. GIS does this by relying on datasets – essentially spreadsheets of data which can be layered together digitally to build maps as complex or simple as you like. If information can be tabulated and linked to a physical location, it can be made into a dataset and a GIS-based map. That map can then be changed in a matter of seconds when the underlying data changes, or if the user simply wants to see its information in a different way.

More complex GIS maps tend to draw from multiple datasets and show how they relate. You can use GIS to create a map showing, for instance, how obesity rates correlate with people's proximity to public parks in a city. Or you can use it to create a map showing how a region's flooding levels have changed over time, with reference to annual temperatures, extreme weather incidents and agricultural practices. GIS can help users show and analyse data, support an argument, form a recommendation, set priorities and communicate a point of view.

There's more to GIS than simply building maps by layering datasets, as any cartographer, geographer or other in-depth user will know. Understanding these basic concepts, and learning how to put them to use with ArcGIS or similar software, is enough to get any librarian or student started on an exciting new research project.

Literature review

GIS is not a new subject for the literature of academic librarianship. However, for the purposes of contextualizing our library's experience – and particularly in order to focus the discussion on academic library support of GIS for disciplines not traditionally associated with GIS – it's helpful to highlight some of the most relevant publications in recent years.

Recent comprehensive studies of GIS in academic libraries include Michalec and Welsh's (2007) survey of the literature from 1990 to 2005 and Abresch et al.'s 2008 title, *Integrating Geographic Information Systems into Library Services*, which provides broad-ranging recommendations for academic libraries seeking to include GIS support in their suite of services. Numerous articles have since examined different aspects of GIS support in libraries, including open-source GIS software, deploying census data in GIS and using GIS as a system to analyse geospatial data in academic library databases (cf. Donnelly, 2010; Hertel and Sprague, 2007; Sedighi, 2012). As of 2015, the literature of GIS in academic libraries is rich and varied, but for the purposes of this discussion the most relevant work is that which discusses support for

GIS in fields outside the traditional core disciplines of geography and urban planning.

What types of GIS support are academic libraries most likely to provide to their users? In 2014, Ann Holstein conducted an online survey of 115 Association of Research Libraries member libraries to determine their range of support for GIS. Of the 54 libraries that responded to the survey, 100% offered access to GIS technology including ArcGIS, Google Earth and Google Maps. According to Holstein's findings, 'Nearly all (94%) [responding] libraries provide assistance using the software for specific class assignments and projects, and 78% are able to provide more in-depth research project consultations' (Holstein, 2015, 43). A majority of responding libraries provided basic GIS software instruction, while fewer provide help with technical issues such as installing the software and managing extensions. Almost half provided some kind of 'virtual training courses and tutorials' (Holstein, 2015, 44).

Perhaps most interesting for the current discussion are Holstein's disciplinary findings, which indicate the prevalence of library-supported GIS use across academic fields. Her results are surprising. While urban planning and geography figure prominently, they rank below environmental studies and almost on par with biology/ecology and geology. Close behind are history, architecture, political science, public health and epidemiology, and sociology. Clearly, the use of GIS is widespread beyond the core cluster of traditional disciplines associated with the tool.

There is a dearth of literature about how academic librarians are stepping in to support the GIS needs of these non-traditional disciplines. But outside the literature of academic libraries it is possible to find at least some examples of the types of GIS work occurring in non-traditional fields, which helps to contextualize the need for library support in this area.

Although Holstein's study finds that use of GIS is low in social work, Felke (2014) provides an example of how GIS is used in the social work curriculum at a college in the north-eastern USA, and comments that the 'use of mapping in social work is not necessarily a new idea' (Felke, 2014, 82). Social workers have historically used maps to quickly show neighbourhood demographics and evaluate services, as well as to study longitudinal changes in communities and make predictions and decisions about programs (Felke, 2014, 83). Felke's assessment of a new credit-bearing GIS course for social work students showed that 74% anticipated using the tool in their professional practice, and that 'comments about the course itself were unanimously positive' (86).

Luebbering's study of GIS in linguistics explores how language policy and practice may be represented through maps, noting that '[l]anguage maps occupy a precarious existence; they are useful and informative, but are rather problematic to create' (Luebbering, 2013, 40) due to the difficulty of representing the fluid realities of language in the severe, literal symbology of vector maps. GIS can help linguists build more complexity and flexibility into language maps, since '[a] single GIS project provides access to multiple map possibilities and views, not just one static product' (50).

MacDonald and Black (2000) discuss the use of GIS in the field of print culture studies – otherwise known as the history of the book – to analyse many aspects of print history. 'For historians of the book, a spatial and temporal framework is . . . important due to the geographic growth of factors such as literacy through time, as well as the mobility of agents of print culture (printers, etc.)' (MacDonald and Black, 2000, 510). They advocate the use of GIS to allow print culture researchers to analyse spatial and temporary data simultaneously or in various combinations, increasing the complexity of the research and allowing new conclusions to be drawn. In other words, 'GIS technology, owing to its capacity to link information from disparate source databases, offers substantial potential for the examination of various print culture assumptions' (MacDonald and Black, 2000, 516).

While geography, cartography and urban studies and planning may be the disciplines most often associated with the use of GIS, it's clear that many other fields of study and research stand to benefit from it. Scholars of all types use GIS to analyse, evaluate, predict and recombine data in new ways. Academic libraries serving multiple disciplines may therefore consider it their responsibility to develop and maintain at least basic staff expertise of GIS as part of the library's suite of research support services. Librarians can play an important role in helping make faculty and students aware of the availability of GIS tools, and of their potential for conducting research in new ways.

GIS in our library

The University of Oregon's (UO) Portland Library and Learning Commons supports a small population of students and faculty in programmes including architecture, journalism, digital arts, law, and product design. Most programmes are at the master's level, and the total student population is currently around 200, with some variation as students migrate between Portland and the main campus in Eugene, over 100 miles away. Many faculty are adjunct (part-time or non-permanent) rather than tenure-track or tenured (permanent). This is a specialized set of professionally oriented academic programmes, serving busy users who are often working or interning at least part-time alongside their studies.

Within this context, the Portland Library supports not only traditional library services, but also academic technology, including videoconference and classroom audiovisual systems, as well as a large-format printing and scanning service. We have a small professional staff, with 1.75 FTE librarians and 3.0 technology specialists. All staff are challenged to provide services in a variety of areas, and to collaborate with specialist colleagues on the main campus.

What we did

Beginning around 2009, the Portland Library began to explore opportunities to support users interested in GIS. The UO Libraries provides access to ArcGIS, the leading national GIS software, via all of its computer workstations in both Eugene and Portland. Thanks to a campus-wide licence, we also offer UO users the ability to install their own copy of the software for free. Further, our map collection includes a subscription to quarterly updates of the Regional Land Information System (RLIS) datasets for the Portland metro area. These datasets include streets, building outlines, tax lots, transit lines and many other features that allow users to quickly draw highly accurate, configurable maps of the Portland area. While we don't subscribe to datasets for other areas, it's possible to find many of them freely available online, so users aren't restricted only to using ArcGIS for Portland-based projects.

It became apparent to Portland Library staff that the UO's Portland-based programmes – particularly our master's architecture students – could make good use of GIS if they were aware of it and had basic instruction in using it. However, while the UO Libraries houses an estimable map, GIS, and aerial photography collection in Eugene, and employs a full-time map librarian, there is no GIS or map specialist position at Portland, and the two sites are over 100 miles apart. None of our Portland staff had experience using ArcGIS, and the software was not taught to students in any of our Portland department curricula.

Portland Library staff began an informal process of learning to use ArcGIS, in order to understand its potential and share our knowledge with users. At first we relied heavily on the online documentation provided by Esri, the company that publishes ArcGIS, as well as on YouTube tutorials and other free online instruction created by users. We also drew on the experience and knowledge of our map librarian colleague in Eugene. We began to discuss GIS with the architecture faculty and students, and then offered some low-threshold, drop-in tutorials in ArcGIS. These were well attended, encouraging us to continue to expend effort in this area.

As we continued to work in this area, we developed our understanding of GIS's concrete applications for architecture students. Most architecture students take a studio class each term, focusing on a single project from ideation through finished design. Many of these projects address real-world architectural design challenges in Portland neighbourhoods, on sites which the students visit in person to photograph, film and sketch.

An early stage in most of their studio projects is the site design or site plan – an overhead view of their project location showing relevant features such as streets, surrounding buildings, sidewalks, curbs, transit lines, street trees, etc. Without access to an accurate map, students resort to drawing these plans themselves, or to sketching over digital images from Google Maps or Google Earth. We learned that a major benefit of GIS to our architecture users was its ability to provide a quick, precise and highly customizable base map which they could then export to design software in order to show site plans in their early and mid-term review.

Over the next several years, Portland Library staff continued to provide informal instruction in ArcGIS, focusing mainly on showing architecture students where and how to access the software and datasets they needed for site design. For more in-depth instruction in using ArcGIS, we engaged the help of adjunct faculty who were familiar with it and willing to demonstrate its use. However, it became clear that this model was not stable and sustainable enough, given GIS's obvious value for our users. In spring 2012, therefore, I enrolled in a four-credit graduate-level GIS course within Portland State University's highly ranked urban studies programme, with the goal of bringing ArcGIS expertise within the library.

Over the course of ten weeks, I delved into much more detail in GIS, beginning with a foundational understanding of mapmaking basics such as projections and co-ordinate systems and progressing through best practices in using ArcGIS. I learned how to create colour-coded choropleth maps, how to geocode and fill in missing street address information, and how to perform more advanced mapping tasks such as searching for particular features within maps, performing calculations on datasets, and editing map features.

I was given work release hours to complete the course, with tuition remission funded by the UO Libraries. Effectively, the quarter-long course gave me the same basic-to-intermediate understanding of GIS that Portland State University gives its graduate planning students. Much of the course content far exceeded the routine demands of the architecture students we serve at the Portland Library, but it was a huge benefit to understand the software and the larger systems of GIS at a conceptual level, and not simply at a procedural one. Many of the more complex and high-level skills have since come in handy in answering students' questions about GIS.

Current GIS services

Since I completed this course, we have offered ArcGIS introductory workshops for architecture students at least quarterly. For each workshop we have created and posted signage, updating it quarterly to keep it fresh, and often taking an irreverent and colourful approach in order to catch the eyes of our busy students. For instance, we styled one quarter's promotional posters to look like metal band posters, complete with Gothic font and flames licking the side of the page. In other terms we used bright orange and blue and a modern sans-serif font to snag our design-conscious students. We promoted these sessions on our library's Facebook page, which has approximately 350 likes as of April 2015, and which regularly receives high 'reach' counts for its posts. We remind students and faculty again via their own internal e-mail newsletter, sent out each week by department staff, and we inform all architecture students about the workshops at their in-person orientation session on the first day of each quarter.

Our most successful classes have been bolstered by the support of architecture faculty encouraging their students to attend – when one influential instructor told his students it was an important skill to learn, we had a standing-room-only session. We also reach a considerable number of students through one-on-one consultations with students. Even students who attend the workshops are inclined to seek out a consultation session. While some students are willing and able to take the time to become comfortable using GIS alone, most use it minimally as a means to an end, and need help remembering how to complete tasks after the initial workshop introduction.

In addition to teaching students how to use ArcGIS, we help students understand the larger context of using GIS in their research projects. We give advice on sourcing GIS datasets for locations beyond the Portland area (which are the only datasets we subscribe to as a campus). As part of our introduction to ArcGIS, we explain what shapefiles are, and demonstrate how to do a Google search for a .shp file type, paired with keywords such as *data*, *GIS*, *catalog*, and *download*. We explain that there is no global standard for providing access to GIS datasets, and that some locations may provide generous free access while others may charge. We suggest that students try searching not only by the name of a city, but also by its county or region, and by agencies such as transit authorities, development commissions and assessors' offices. We also remind students that some parts of the world – rural areas, developing countries, countries whose language the student doesn't speak or read – are more challenging places to source GIS data for than others. We help students conduct searches for GIS data for sites ranging from Seattle to Jerusalem – and are often successful in helping find data they can't, either by changing search strategies or by taking the direct route of contacting a government agency with a request for educational data.

In order to supplement our in-person workshops and consultations, we created a series of online tutorials that document the most common ArcGIS tasks our students approach. These tutorials cover topics such as accessing our licensed datasets on our university server; creating maps using different feature layers; interpreting data in attribute tables; changing map symbology; cropping maps (an important task, since exporting an entire metro area's worth of data will crash the software); and exporting files to design software such as AutoCAD and Revit. The tutorials are currently hosted on Google Documents for ease of editing, since they make use of many screenshots that are time-consuming to upload and format in our Drupal-based website. This arrangement may change as our library migrates our research guides to LibGuides over summer 2015.

In spring 2015 our technology services manager and I were asked to provide more in-depth GIS support for an adjunct faculty member teaching an architecture course on digital tools and methods. While only part of his course dealt with GIS, we were pleased to be recognized as a local authority on the topic, and to be included in his course planning as a result. We offered his students multiple hands-on tutorial and lab sessions, assisting them with installing the software on their personal laptops and accessing the campus licence, downloading datasets, building their maps, and modelling their neighbourhood sites in 3D using ArcScene, a new ArcGIS skill learned by our technology services manager specifically to support this class.

In this case, the course instructor was interested in moving beyond the creation of simple site plan maps and into more analytic use of the software to encourage students to envision floor area ratios, transit routes, neighbourhood destinations, traffic patterns and more. Some of his ambitions required more intermediate-level and in-depth knowledge of both ArcGIS and our regional datasets, and so working with the class required careful preparation and communication with GIS professionals and advisors such as Portland city planners. We were pleased to be invited to visit subsequent classes, which included translating GIS layers into data for Grasshopper – a graphic algorithm plug-in for 3D modelling software Rhino – and producing the types of financial prediction documents used by commercial real estate developers. This was an excellent illustration of the potential of GIS to help our architecture students and faculty do exciting, real-world research.

Disciplinary reach of GIS

Architecture is currently the UO's largest academic programme in Portland, and has so far shown the most interest in learning and applying GIS skills to the curriculum. But our library also serves master's students in the college of journalism, in both strategic communication and multimedia (production, documentary) journalism. Both of these departments could make good use of GIS, given knowledge of its capabilities. Multimedia students working on documentary shorts can use GIS to create clear visual representations of spatial data such as neighbourhood income levels, racial and cultural demographics, and so on. Strategic communication students working on reports and marketing plans can use GIS to show how consumer demographics play out in local (or national) areas.

Anecdotally, students in both journalism programmes have expressed interest in learning how to use ArcGIS, but most were unable to attend the introductory workshop we offered due to schedule conflicts. Many of the students in the journalism department work full- or part-time, attending classes on evenings and over the weekend. Most are only in our building for classes, and have little spare time for extra-curricular learning projects.

In the winter 2015 quarter I made an overture to two faculty members in the journalism programme, inviting them and their students to take advantage of our ArcGIS expertise. Through this conversation, we learned that the journalism programme would soon be offering a course on data visualization methods that would include GIS, and that the library might be able to help support that course. We continue to promote GIS to our journalism users through our monthly e-newsletter for their discipline, as well as through library displays, our Facebook page, and via mentions in classroom visits. As of spring 2015 we are still in conversation about how the library can best support journalism students and faculty, particularly during terms when the data visualization class isn't offered.

Outcomes

Since we started offering support for GIS research activities, we have seen a substantial rise in the use of GIS and in expectations around how GIS is supported in our library. At a minimum, architecture students who might previously have sketched or traced their site plans now regularly use ArcGIS to create accurate and current building outlines. Many students push farther, using the software to create complex, multi-layered maps showing many different types of data.

Attendance at our training workshops has varied widely, from more than 20 participants to as few as two or three. Some of this variance probably stems from the curriculum and class scheduling conflicts – with such a small, homogenous user group a single major schedule conflict can scuttle an entire session. However, even in terms when our drop-in GIS workshops are poorly attended, we continue to see many in-person requests for consultation and in-person instruction, and ArcGIS instruction remains a consistently high priority for our users on our annual technology survey.

Our own staff expertise has expanded due to our commitment to providing GIS support for our users. Two staff members – myself and our technology manager – are confident troubleshooting basic mapping problems, and other staff are trained to refer to our online tutorials. We have developed relationships with regional dataset providers, to understand the finer details of the data we use. Staff receive regular current awareness e-mails from our data providers, and have attended in-person continuing education events that they offer.

We are gratified to see that students and faculty consider us an authoritative resource for GIS instruction, as evidenced by our inclusion in class planning and delivery of the new digital methods architecture course. While our outcomes have been less substantial for our journalism users, we have a solid footing from which to continue our promotion and awareness-building efforts.

Finally, our support of GIS for architecture in particular has given us more and better insight into the curriculum and our users. We understand better the types of assignments that students do, and their specific interests and needs. We've learned about their digital workflows and we know more about the gaps in their digital literacy, simply from watching them work and answering their questions. Supporting GIS has bolstered our reputation among architecture students and faculty; we are not viewed as simply a repository for books and magazines, but as individuals with valuable expertise we're willing to share. Many of them know our faces and names – and vice versa – because of the GIS support we offer.

Lessons learned

Our most significant lesson learned may be that supporting GIS in a small remote branch library requires substantial staff investment, not only in pursuing datasets and training staff to use software, but in updating our skills and awareness as new tools emerge and even in promoting the tool to faculty and students. If we had more staff time to give to GIS support we could easily develop our services in this area to include far more service and promote the tool more assertively to a wider range of users. Our primary limitation in adding more GIS support is staff time.

While supporting GIS is resource-intensive, especially in a small branch library, it appears to be well worth it. Our staff find it satisfying to fill this need, and our users respond with enthusiasm and gratitude. However, we've learned that we must be clear about our limited ability to support other types of software at this level. The UO Libraries also provides access to Adobe Creative Cloud software on our academic workstations, as well as statistical modelling software and other tools intended to support a wide range of disciplines. Staff do not train students how to use this software, either in Eugene or in Portland. Arguably, the Portland Library could choose to develop staff expertise in, for instance, Adobe Photoshop, in order to answer student questions and provide workshops and consultations that would improve our users' experience of the library. But we simply lack the staff, funding and budget to support all of the software we provide.

We made a strategic decision to develop expertise in ArcGIS because it is a specialized piece of software that students and faculty were unlikely to explore on their own, because in Portland we lack access to a map librarian's expertise, and because we felt GIS had a demonstrable relationship to our collections (licensed datasets) and services (research and reference). In an ideal world we would offer a similar level of support for the many different kinds of design software we offer, which are also used across disciplines. However, while most students seem familiar with Adobe Creative Suite when they enter our programmes, and many have used Photoshop and InDesign on their own, very few know much about GIS and its potential. We felt that students were unlikely to understand the concepts underlying GIS without some hands-on training and support, and we thought it was also unlikely that the academic departments would ever offer a consistent course in GIS software and concepts in our remote location. This all made ArcGIS support seem like a relatively 'quick win' for the library, especially since GIS is by its very nature closely tied to research and resources that are already core to the library's mission. We try to be very clear with our users that our GIS support is not mandated by official UO Libraries policy, and that we cannot support our entire image of software as fully as we do ArcGIS.

What's next

Some of our goals, which we must prioritize according to our many other projects, include:

- *Continue to build staff expertise.* We recently began to explore ArcScene, an element of ArcGIS which has the ability to show map elements in 3D. This is a popular feature for architecture users in particular, who often want to show their site context in three dimensions. In addition, we would like to build our understanding of how ArcGIS can work with Rhino (3D modelling software) and its many plug-ins and add-ons. City Builder, another piece of mapping software that focuses on building city profiles according to variables provided by users, is also of interest. Finally, as free open-source GIS tools like Open Streets and Google Earth become more sophisticated and widely available, we would like to learn how they can serve our users' GIS needs.
- *Continue to expand our user group.* As more University of Oregon (UO) programmes build their presence in Portland, we expect to invite new users to investigate the potential of using GIS. Programmes like historic

preservation, law, digital arts and product design are all scheduled to build or grow in Portland, and all could use GIS in their curricula. In particular, we would like to see more use among journalism students and faculty. We can accomplish this by promoting the ways that GIS can help tell stories and show data in strong, convincing, visual ways. Faculty are key in the effort to expand GIS awareness to journalism users, because journalism students are rarely in the building and are harder to reach than students in our studio-based programmes such as architecture and product design.

- *Explore opportunities to create GIS-themed displays and exhibits.* Our library regularly hosts exhibitions of student work including photography, architectural boards, drawings and design. We can add a strongly visual GIS exhibit to demonstrate the power of GIS across disciplines.
- *Explore opportunities to host a speaker on a GIS theme or topic.* Particularly in co-ordination with known GIS-based courses, we can investigate speakers from our Regional Land Information System office, or from local firms or other universities in the Portland area.
- *Help build awareness of GIS among non-map librarians.* We would like to help overcome the sense that GIS is too specialized for academic librarians to support. We can promote our own efforts in this area to our colleagues in Eugene and at other institutions, highlighting the potential for GIS to enrich research across many disciplines. And we can engage the help of our UO Libraries map librarian as an ambassador for GIS in both Eugene and Portland.

References and further reading

Abresch, J., Hanson, A., Heron, S. J. and Reehling, P. J. (2008) *Integrating Geographic Information Systems into Library Services: a guide for academic libraries.* Hershey, PA, Information Science Publishing.

Donnelly, F. P. (2010) Evaluating Open Source GIS for Libraries, *Library Hi Tech,* **28** (1), 131–51.

Felke, T. P. (2014) Building Capacity for the Use of Geographic Information Systems (GIS) in Social Work Planning, Practice, and Research, *Journal of Technology in Human Services,* **32** (1/2), 81–92.

Hertel, K. and Sprague, N. (2007) GIS and Census Data: tools for library planning, *Library Hi Tech,* **25** (2), 246–59.

Holstein, A. L. (2015) Geographic Information and Technologies in Academic Libraries: an ARL survey of services and support, *Information Technology & Libraries,* **34** (1), 38–51.

Luebbering, C. (2013) Displaying the Geography of Language: the cartography of language maps, *Linguistics Journal,* **7** (1), 39–67.

MacDonald, B. H. and Black, F. A. (2000) Using GIS for Spatial and Temporal Analyses in Print Culture Studies, *Social Science History*, **24** (3), 505–36.

Michalec, M. and Welsh, T. S. (2007) Quantity and Authorship of GIS Articles in Library and Information Science Literature, 1990–2005, *Science & Technology Libraries*, **27**, 65–77.

Pournaghi, R. and Babalhavaeji, F. (2015) The Factors and Criteria for Prioritization of GIS Utilization by Libraries, *Electronic Library*, **33** (2), 181–95.

Sedighi, M. (2012) Application of Geographic Information System (GIS) in Analyzing Geospatial Information of Academic Library Databases, *The Electronic Library*, **30** (3), 367–76.

Research as a conversation

PART 3

Research as a consultation

Introduction to Part 3

Starr Hoffman

The idea of research as a conversation

In 1941, Kenneth Burke was the first to use the metaphor of 'research as a conversation':

> Imagine that you enter a parlor. You come late. When you arrive, others have long preceded you, and they are engaged in a heated discussion, a discussion too heated for them to pause and tell you exactly what it is about. In fact, the discussion had already begun long before any of them got there, so that no one present is qualified to retrace for you all the steps that had gone before. You listen for a while, until you decide that you have caught the tenor of the argument; then you put in your oar. Someone answers; you answer him; another comes to your defense; another aligns himself against you, to either the embarrassment or gratification of your opponent, depending upon the quality of your ally's assistance. However, the discussion is interminable. The hour grows late, you must depart. And you do depart, with the discussion still vigorously in progress.
>
> Burke, 1974

Although this metaphor is not new in academia, it persists because it is a succinct and accurate description of the ideal of building knowledge. The phrase describes new knowledge as not a 'eureka'-like bolt of lightning out of a clear summer sky, but rather as something built upon the solid foundation of pre-existing research. Whether the existing research agrees with established research or questions and refutes it, it is clearly situated in the established research conversation. This metaphor touches on several key aspects of libraries: providing access to previous research, educating users in how to discover it and give credit to it, and helping students learn how to analyse, synthesize and respond to it.

This metaphor is complemented in 1962 by Thomas Kuhn's seminal work on research, *The Structure of Scientific Revolutions* (Kuhn, 1970), which describes paradigm-shifting moments in scientific research. Kuhn's view of the history of science challenged the then-popular view that science was merely an inevitable accumulation of facts over time leading to a single, coherent framework. Instead, Kuhn pointed out how scientific anomalies that don't fit into the existing framework (what Kuhn called the 'dominant paradigm') can lead to requestioning old data with new hypotheses (a period he called 'scientific revolution') and ultimately to a new paradigm.

One of Kuhn's famous examples deals with astronomy. He describes how Copernicus set out to explain observed scientific anomalies by developing a new cosmology centred around the Sun. However, Kuhn explains that because Copernican cosmology didn't support the existing data any better than the dominant paradigm, the Ptolemaic Earth-centric view, it was rejected in his time. Only after Galileo and Kepler illustrated enough supporting evidence and additional theories to explain further anomalies was Copernican cosmology shown to be a better, less complex paradigm to explain planetary orbits than Ptolemaic cosmology.

Kuhn's example provides a rich illustration of the importance of research as a conversation. Kepler was not operating in a vacuum, he was exploring and questioning the established Ptolemaic paradigm and existing data (from Copernicus, Galileo and others) through a new point of view, with different assumptions than scientists before him. Kuhn shows that research as a conversation can produce both 'normal science' (in which current research builds on previous research without questioning its assumptions) and 'scientific revolution' (in which the dominant paradigm is rejected after re-examination of previous research through the new paradigm). To expand this concept of 'normal science' to other disciplines, let us call this earlier period 'normal research'. Thus, to support both normal research and paradigm-shifting revolutions, libraries must be a vital part of this conversation.

Supporting the research conversation in libraries

How do libraries support this research conversation? Traditionally, a fundamental aspect of research support has been collecting existing research and preserving it for later access by scholars. Over decades and even centuries, this has produced research libraries across the world with rich but also staggeringly vast physical collections which are difficult to continue to sustain. Interlibrary loan services and consortium agreements, which have long been a part of the library landscape, are expanding with greater reliance on co-operative collecting and lending in order to continue to provide scholars with access to rich collections, while relieving some of the burden on individual libraries. Additionally, the growing presence of research online has refocused some attention from collecting physical books and journals to providing access to online journals, e-books and other methods of research dissemination, such as through social media.

Dissemination

The traditional path to dissemination for scholars has been (allowing for some variance between disciplines) first a poster describing a proposed or in-progress research project, then an academic paper presented to a limited audience and finally a publication (as either a journal article or a monograph) available to a broader audience. However, even the final article or book was typically limited in its reach to an academic audience, rather than the general public. This limitation is often due in part to cost, considering that in many fields, academic publications are far more costly per volume than a book one might purchase in a common bookstore. The volume's cost and academic scope therefore further limits which bookstores carry it and which libraries collect it, in turn further limiting its potential audience to those with access to academic libraries instead of public libraries.

The internet itself has broken down some of these barriers because of its inherent ability to let anyone produce and disseminate content, potentially worldwide. However, the true revolution in public access to research has been the development of the open access (OA) movement.

Open access at its heart is a movement about making research more available; it has taken research out of the tightly controlled realm of academic publishing. This has provided academic authors with more copyright control over their work and has made research available outside of academia. One of the most democratic outcomes of the movement has been changes in federal research funding requirements in the USA, resulting in public access to research that is supported by federal – taxpayer – dollars (Center for Digital Research and Scholarship, 2015). One of the best known success stories of open access has been the story of a high school sophomore, who by reading open access research was able to develop a pancreatic cancer diagnostic that is cheaper, faster and more accurate than the existing options (Right to Research Coalition, n.d., c. 2013). If the research he had used had not been published through open access, this high school student would not have had access to that valuable information. School libraries typically can't afford costly subscriptions to individual science journals or to databases aggregating scientific research.

Developments in open access have provided many different ways that libraries can support this new research realm. The aforementioned federal funding requirements have brought with them the need to assist faculty with grant proposals, particularly with the creation of data management plans

(DMPs). These plans provide details about how data resulting from the research will be collected, kept secure, shared with others, and ultimately preserved and archived. In some cases, libraries also serve as the place where this data will be shared (through institutional repositories), described (by creating metadata), discovered (through systems such as repositories and library catalogues) and archived (on servers or other means).

Library support for sharing research outcomes through open access can extend to traditional forms of research dissemination as well, through journals and books. This support may be simple, such as making faculty aware of options to retain copyright to their work – including the right to make pre-prints available on their personal websites for free – by submitting addendums like SPARC's *Author Addendum* with their copyright agreements to traditional academic publishers (SPARC, 2006). Another simple method is making faculty aware of the broad variety of open access journals in which they can publish, including the renowned *PloS One* journal of science.

Additional forms of library support may include committing funds or staff time. For instance, some libraries provide grants to fund faculty publication in 'gold access' journals, in which the up-front cost of publication is paid by authors and other participants, so that the final work is made freely available to the public. Some libraries even host or create original open access journals for their institution, providing server space and other contributions, such as expert knowledge. Others preserve research and related conversations found in blogs, tweets, and other non-traditional outlets, and some provide consultation services to assist faculty seeking tenure in tracking the impact of these outputs using altmetrics.

The fundamental goal with open access is to disseminate research broadly, to make faculty's contributions widely accessible, thus allowing their work to impact the scholarly conversation.

Discovery

It is difficult to talk about dissemination without talking about discovery, as they are interlocking concepts. The act of making research accessible by disseminating it also necessitates other methods of making it discoverable. Traditionally, this work has been invisible to scholars, as it was performed behind the scenes. Publishers and vendors created print indexes to journals that became citation databases and finally combined with the original articles they described in full-text databases. Now instead of consulting separate print indexes to find articles on a topic, scholars primarily use these integrated databases to search for keywords and subject terms that seamlessly take them to linked articles. Similarly, librarians catalogue books and other resources to make them discoverable through the library catalogue, assigning subject headings and abstracts. Even when faculty publish in open access journals, it is often these same systems that catalogue and index their work.

However, for some of these new methods of dissemination there are not yet consistent workflows. For instance, submitting an article or dataset to an institutional repository entails very different workflows, depending on the institution. In some cases, faculty submit the work themselves, in others librarians actively seek out faculty work to add, and some combine these methods. Apart from the submission of the content itself is the creation of its metadata, which is integral to making the content discoverable within the repository and across the internet.

Similar to the submission of content, creating metadata is an activity that is sometimes left to faculty themselves, sometimes entirely to librarians and sometimes to a partnership between the two. Partnerships themselves take various forms. Some libraries offer workshops to teach faculty and research assistants how to create descriptive, effective metadata for their work, while others provide consultation models in which librarians and faculty create the metadata co-operatively.

Regardless of how it is created and by whom, quality metadata is integral to making research findable, thus ensuring that it becomes a part of the scholarly conversation.

Education

The previous sections described how to make research a part of the conversation. However, another integral part of keeping the scholarly conversation alive is to train new scholars in the research process (David-Kahl, Fishel and Hensley, 2014). Scholars are not born, but made – they must be shown how to find research, trained in how to consume and question it and provided with the critical thinking skills to reach their own conclusions and participate in the conversation themselves. All of these activities are part of information literacy instruction, a vital service in many academic libraries.

Often, undergraduates starting their college education conceive of the research paper as an exercise in regurgitation. When assigned a topic, they produce something more akin to an annotated bibliography, a paper that lists and summarizes the minimal number of sources required by their assignment. The task, then, for the instruction librarian is not only to show them how to navigate the library's discovery systems, but also how to analyse and evaluate various sources, to critically engage with the work, and to properly give credit to the work of previous scholars. The scale of this task, particularly given that instruction is often limited to a single interaction with students that may not even span a full class session, cannot be overstated.

There are multiple tools and mnemonics for teaching students about critical engagement, including the 'research as a conversation' metaphor itself. A recent tool is Joseph Bizup's BEAM (2008), which divides sources into four categories based on their usefulness to the scholar: background (provides basic facts), exhibits (sources to be analysed or interpreted), arguments (discourse of the topic, the essence of the scholarly conversation) and method (source using similar analysis or terminology). The BEAM method shows students how to engage with sources in a variety of ways, illustrating that sources can be used for different purposes. This encourages students to move beyond their typical understanding of sources as background only. The Association of College and Research Libraries' recently released *Framework for Information Literacy for Higher Education* (2015) is a framework upon which information literacy instructors can develop instruction plans and assess student learning outcomes. The framework provides six concepts central to information literacy, including 'research as inquiry' and 'scholarship as a conversation.'

Recasting discovery and citation as integral parts of the scholarly conversation can elevate these activities beyond the traditional library instruction method of teaching the library catalogue and style manuals as required skills. Discovery, as discussed earlier, can be described as how students enter the scholarly conversation and listen. Citation is important as a method for students to give credit to those scholars who shaped their own argument, as well as points the way to those scholars for anyone who later reads the student's work. It is not only the student's argument itself that contributes to the conversation, but also their analysis, synthesis and citation of previous scholarship.

In an effort to streamline instruction and fully address all these tasks, librarians have explored new delivery models for information literacy. Some libraries have successfully lobbied for information literacy to be added to the core curriculum, creating standalone courses (sometimes credit-bearing) that address the topic over the length of a semester. Others have assigned 'personal librarians' to classes or student groups based on subject familiarity, residential housing (dormitory or residential librarians) or online presence (embedded librarians as instructors or assistants in online and blended courses). Physically embedding librarians in academic departments can enrich relationships not only with faculty but also with students, providing additional opportunities for librarians to both teach information literacy in faculty classes and to meet individually with students on these topics. Standalone online courses in information literacy are another option; one of the following chapters details creating an information literacy MOOC.

Regardless of the method, training students – the scholars of the next generation – how to find, cite and interact with existing research is integral to the persistence of the academy and the creation of new knowledge. The following chapters will detail three key examples of supporting the scholarly conversation through dissemination, discovery and education.

References

Association of College and Research Libraries (ACRL) (2015) *Framework for Information Literacy for Higher Education*, www.ala.org/acrl/sites/ala.org.acrl/files/content/issues/infolit/Framework_ILHE.pdf.

Bizup, J. (2008) BEAM: a rhetorical vocabulary for teaching research-based writing, *Rhetoric Review*, **27** (1), 72–86.

Burke, K. (1974) *The Philosophy of Literary Form: studies in symbolic action*, 3rd edn, Berkeley, CA, University of California Press.

Center for Digital Research and Scholarship (2015) Public Access Mandates for Federally Funded Research: implementation plans, *Scholarly Communication Program*, Center for Digital Research and Scholarship, Columbia University Libraries/Information Services, http://scholcomm.columbia.edu/open-access/public-access-mandates-for-federally-funded-research.

David-Kahl, S., Fishel, T. A. and Hensley, M. K. (2014) Weaving the Threads: scholarly communication and information literacy, *C&RL News*, **75** (8), 441–4, http://crln.acrl.org/content/75/8/441.full.

Kuhn, T. S. (1970) *The Structure of Scientific Revolutions*, 2nd edn, Chicago, IL, University of Chicago Press.

Right to Research Coalition. (n.d., c. 2013) *16-year-old Touts Role of Open Access in Breakthrough Cancer Diagnostic: interview of Jack Andraka by Dr Francis Collins, Director of the NIH*, Scholarly Publishing and Academic Resources Coalition, www.sparc.arl.org/news/16-year-old-touts-role-open-access-breakthrough-cancer-diagnostic-interview-jack-andraka-dr.

SPARC (2006) *Author Addendum*, Scholarly Publishing and Academic Resources Coalition, www.sparc.arl.org/resources/authors/addendum.

CHAPTER 7

Implementing open access across a large university: a case study

Dominic Tate

Introduction and context

Edinburgh University Library is in the midst of undertaking a programme to facilitate the widespread adoption of open access (OA) to journal articles and conference proceedings across the entire University, in line with current UK higher education funding council policy.

Over the last few years there has been a significant increase in the number of institutional and research-funder policies mandating OA research results, taking advantage of both green and gold routes. In the UK, academic institutions and research centres have tended to mandate green OA, which is achieved by self-archiving into a repository. UK research funders have recognized that it is their responsibility not only to fund the original research, but also to ensure the widest possible dissemination of its results. For that reason, some funders do not limit their policies to green OA, but also extend them to gold OA, and take responsibility for covering gold article-processing charges (APCs) when they arise.

OA policy in the UK is evolving very rapidly, and in 2013 it was announced that from 2016, journal articles and conference proceedings must be deposited in a repository and made OA wherever this is possible (subject to publisher embargo), otherwise they would not be eligible for future research assessment exercises. For the first time in the UK, this policy has linked the OA agenda with research assessment – something which may have implications for university funding – and this has significantly increased the importance of OA to universities.

In this context, institutions need to work quickly to raise awareness of OA and to increase compliance with research-funder policies. The pace of change has increased significantly and universities are working to tight deadlines to ensure as many of their journal articles and conference proceedings as possible are eligible for assessment.

Background to open access in the UK and at the University of Edinburgh

There are approximately 110 universities in the UK, with the overwhelming majority (including all of the major research-intensive institutions) publicly funded through government grants.

Open access has been on the higher education agenda in the UK since the early 2000s, though it was a relatively low priority until 2012. The UK's Joint Information Systems Committee (Jisc) encouraged universities to adopt institutional repositories (IRs) via a number of initiatives in the early- and mid-2000s such as the London EPrints Access Project and the Repositories Support Project (Jisc, n.d., Jisc, 2009). By the end of the decade, most UK universities had their own IRs, but academic usage and general acceptance of open access by academics remained low.

The University of Edinburgh is a large research-led institution based in Scotland's capital city. The University has over 32,000 students and 12,000 staff, and is a member of the Russell Group, the League of European Research Universities (LERU), and Universitas 21. Edinburgh was a relatively early adopter of open access, having adopted its initial DSpace Institutional Repository (Edinburgh Research Archive, www.era.lib.ed.ac.uk) in 2003, and now has over 36,000 full-text open access research outputs in its systems. This work is facilitated by the Library's Scholarly Communications Team and is supported by the University's Research Publications Policy, which strongly endorses OA, with a stated preference for the green route.

Since 2008, Edinburgh University Library has managed a fund to pay gold APCs to Wellcome Trust-funded authors and managed a number of publisher accounts to make best use of these funds. More recently, this fund has been expanded to cover a number of other UK-based medical charities (Charity Open Access Fund – COAF), and has been complemented by a second, much larger fund to cover APCs for research papers arising from Research Councils UK (RCUK)-funded research. The library only manages these external funds, as the University does not have its own dedicated fund for gold APCs.

From the initiation of both the repository and the gold APC funds, although there were many pockets of enthusiasm, OA did not become part of the fabric of academic life across all disciplines in the way many in the library had hoped. Academic culture did not shift significantly or rapidly towards either OA model.

In 2011 the University of Edinburgh adopted Atira's PURE CRIS (now an Elsevier product), and this is also used as the primary repository for new peer-reviewed published research outputs.

More recently, additional funder OA policies and initiatives such as those of the Wellcome Trust, FP7 and Horizon 2020 have helped to raise awareness of OA issues (European Commission, 2015; Wellcome Trust, n.d.). However, despite fairly wide publicity since the introduction of the repository, habitual uptake of open access options by University of Edinburgh authors has only really become part of everyday academic practice in some scientific and medical disciplines – a fairly typical scenario in most UK universities.

Open access policy in the UK

In 2012, Research Councils UK (RCUK) strengthened its existing open access policy, effectively requiring that journal articles and conference proceedings arising from research funded by the seven RCUK members are made open access within a maximum 6–24 months from the date of publication, dependent on academic discipline (Research Councils UK, 2014). This policy allows both green and gold OA, though rapid access is preferred, and RCUK has provided block grants to 30 research-led universities for gold OA where publisher embargo periods are too long to meet the RCUK requirements.

The University of Edinburgh responded to this policy by beginning an Open Access Implementation Project, which paid for some staff time to source and upload repository-appropriate copies of journal articles and conference proceedings to its institutional repository (University of Edinburgh, 2015a). This approach was successful, and the University achieved OA rates of 64% for RCUK-funded journal articles and conference proceedings in the first year of the policy – a compliance rate fairly typical of research-led universities in the UK (Tate, 2014).

The Research Excellence Framework (REF) is the current system for assessing the quantity and quality of research undertaken in UK higher education institutions. Following wide consultation, the four UK higher education funding bodies – led by the Higher Education Funding Council for England (HEFCE) – have introduced an open access requirement in the next assessment, referred to as the post-2014 Research Excellence Framework, likely to take place in 2020 (Higher Education Funding Council for England, n.d.). This new requirement comes into effect on 1 April 2016.

The guiding principle of this requirement is that journal articles and conference proceedings must be available in an open access form in order to be eligible for submission to the post-2014 REF. In practice, this means that these outputs must be uploaded to an institutional or subject repository at the point of acceptance for publication. This is a green open access requirement, and even if the author takes a gold route, deposit into a repository must still be made.

The REF assesses the full range of research undertaken at UK universities and research centres and is funder-agnostic. Indeed, in many fields, much of the research assessed is unfunded. The implication of this policy for research-led institutions such as the University of Edinburgh is that all journal articles and conference proceedings will need to be made OA. The deposit requirements are stringent and auditable (full-text documents must be added to a repository immediately on acceptance by the publisher and made open as soon as the publisher allows). Failure to comply presents significant reputational and financial risks, for both researchers and universities. Accordingly, OA is now considered an institutional priority by University management.

The principal way in which the REF OA requirements have changed the landscape in the UK is that they have made OA a priority for all researchers. Previously, it was something which RCUK- and COAF-funded authors *should* do. Now it is something that everyone *must* do. The reasons for this change are twofold. First, researchers could comply with RCUK and COAF policies retrospectively, and there were historically no major sanctions for researcher non-compliance with these policies (though this is also changing). Secondly, REF applies to 'unfunded' research (i.e. research carried out at a UK university but not arising directly from a research grant). These research outputs (often written by staff from arts and humanities disciplines) are eligible for submission to REF but do not come under other research-funder policies. Although such research outputs are not the result of a *direct* research grant award, if we are talking about papers written during the course of employment on university time, then there is a strong argument that these items are also publicly funded.

The University of Edinburgh's approach to implementing open access requirements

The OA requirements for the next REF exercise require deposit to a repository at the *point of acceptance*. This particular aspect of the policy represents perhaps the biggest change to the way universities manage OA. Date of acceptance has not previously been recorded and so new metadata has had to be developed for repository systems in order to capture this information.

Researchers will have to change what they do at the point at which their papers are accepted by a publisher. What is being asked is small – researchers must simply add a document to a repository (or ask someone to do this for them) – but they need to do this within a certain timeframe (a maximum of three months from date of acceptance) and they need to get it right. The implementation of the requirements means that awareness must be raised amongst all university research staff and adequate support needs to be in place to help answer questions and provide support.

From very early on, an assumption was made that as long as the author deposits on acceptance, then repository administrators will be able to ensure compliance with REF *and* funder OA policies, even if they are not complementary.

Edinburgh University Library has chosen to treat the implementation of the REF OA requirements as a project, with a beginning, middle and end. The rationale for adopting a project-based approach is that the University views the adoption of the new requirements as a period of managed change, after which the new processes will become embedded in academic, administrative and library practice, and will become business as usual.

Senior management support for the project from the highest level of the University was essential in giving Edinburgh University Library the authority to implement the plans and to act as a co-ordinating body on behalf of the University's Research Policy Group.

The University of Edinburgh conducts research in a wide range of academic disciplines and is made up of three Colleges (Humanities and Social Sciences, Medicine and Veterinary Medicine and Science and Engineering). Despite a large amount of interdisciplinary research and teaching, each of these Colleges operates independently from the point of view of organizational structure. Within the three Colleges are 22 Schools, based on a number of different campuses in and around the city, housing over 6000 academic staff.

Because of the (by UK standards) large size and devolved structure of the University, the Library took the decision to operate a more decentralized approach to the implementation of OA. During 2013, the University ran a one-year *Open Access Implementation Project*, which employed staff to sit in the 22 Schools and work with academics to explain green OA and help them to upload items to the institutional repository. This project was a great success and resulted in a sharp spike in the number of deposits to the IR. This was attributed to having dedicated staff to handle OA and to these staff being visible in Schools and being closer to academic practice, rather than working remotely from a central library.

The University's Research Policy Group (RPG) agreed for Edinburgh University Library's Scholarly Communications Team to co-ordinate the implementation of the policy centrally within the institution. The Scholarly Communications Team would provide regular updates to RPG detailing progress and rates of compliance with the policy. Although the date of policy implementation is 1 April 2016, the decision was taken to act much earlier to enable time for potential problems to come to light, and for remedial action to be taken if anything does not work as intended.

The Scholarly Communications Team agreed on School-level implementation plans with Humanities and Social Sciences and Science and Engineering, whereas a College-wide approach is being implemented in Medicine and Veterinary Medicine. There are a number of reasons why adopting a devolved approach and agreeing on local implementation plans was felt to be the most useful approach:

- Plans would ideally dovetail neatly with existing academic practice as far as possible.
- Conversations with research leads and administrative staff within individual Schools highlighted issues which library staff alone may not have been able to anticipate.
- The University's IR is also its current research information system (CRIS) – and so submission would be via the CRIS. Local planning would help ensure that we could do everything necessary to engage administrators and academics with the system.

Schools were encouraged to include a simple risk register, communications plan and responsibility matrix into their implementation plans. This helped to facilitate discussions about potential problems, who would be responsible for what, and how the policy would be communicated during the planning phase.

Edinburgh University Library's Scholarly Communications Team is made up of four full-time staff. In addition to this central team, there are a number of additional staff working either full or part-time on open access based in the various Colleges and Schools of the University (at present 6 FTE in total) – though all of these staff are on fixed-term contracts during this period of transition. In addition to this, a number of existing local administrative staff have some responsibility for OA as part of their role (the number of hours these staff contribute to supporting OA is hard to quantify accurately). This generous level of staffing means that there is currently a good level of first-line support in Schools and Colleges for everyday questions about OA and publisher policies. More complex enquiries are escalated to the Scholarly Communications Team in the Library.

Reporting and progress monitoring is an integral part of the programme at the University of Edinburgh, but has also posed some problems. From the very beginning, the scholarly Communications Team realized the importance of being able to provide accurate reports from the CRIS, detailing which publications had been added to the CRIS on a unit-by-unit basis, whether full text was added, and whether the document was added within three months of the date of acceptance (as per the policy). Early inconsistencies in the CRIS data have been improved, but the biggest challenge is knowing what the overall research output of the University should look like. It is quite easy to find the numerator (i.e. the number of OA items added to the repository) but it is much harder to accurately calculate the denominator (the total number of journal articles and conference proceedings published by the University's staff). External services such as Incites and Scopus can help in sciences and medicine, but it is far more difficult to find external sources to provide accurate information on publications in the Arts and Humanities.

Going above and beyond

The REF OA policy covers only journal articles and conference proceedings, because at the time the policy was devised, it was felt that the field of OA monographs was not sufficiently mature for HEFCE to require monographs to be OA in the forthcoming REF. However, the policy also stipulates that additional credit may be available in the Research Environment component of the next REF for universities which can demonstrate that they have gone above and beyond the bare minimum implementation. For this reason, Edinburgh's College of Humanities and Social Sciences has required 100% deposit of *all research outputs* into the CRIS since January 2015. These are then checked and wherever it is possible and suitable to do so, other item types are also made available on an OA basis, including monographs and non-textual research outputs.

Communicating the changes

From the beginning it was acknowledged that communications within a large and decentralized organization can often be challenging. For that reason we preferred to devolve general communications about the policy to individual Schools. Feedback has suggested that this is largely working, though it will be supplemented and reinforced by higher-level communications such as all-staff communications from Heads of Colleges or even the Principal.

Communications plans asked practitioners to consider the different stakeholders (audiences) which need to be reached as well as the messages which need to be communicated (in their simplest form) and the available media for delivering those messages.

Typical communications about the policy include:

- initial e-mail from the head of school regarding the policy
- monthly follow-up reminder e-mails asking if staff have had anything accepted for publication in the last month
- visit to departmental meeting from Scholarly Communications Team
- one-to-one, in-office consultations with publications assistant, local administrator or library representative
- minimum deposit checklist and other simple 'how-to' documentation
- pigeon-hole flyers for all staff during Open Access Week.

Communications are constantly under review, as they are critical to the success of the implementation. Fundamentally, one key message is being broadcast consistently, which is that academics must take some action at the point of acceptance. Depending on whether the School has a mediated deposit or author self-deposit procedure, the message is conveyed as either:

A. 'When you receive an acceptance e-mail, create a record in the IR and upload your author's final peer-reviewed manuscript' OR
B. 'When you receive an acceptance e-mail, forward it on to [dedicated OA inbox] remembering to attach your author's final peer-reviewed manuscript'.

Challenges

Edinburgh University Library has been a proponent of open access for 15 years, and has worked hard over that time to educate researchers about the issues in the current (subscription-based) scholarly communications system. Over that time, the Library has generated a real sense of positivity about OA, although of course there are some staff who are less convinced.

Although research assessment is necessary, it is not something which is always viewed favourably by researchers. It is important to acknowledge that some researchers find research assessment exercises such as the REF time-consuming and bureaucratic, and they often are not viewed in a positive light. Associating open access with research assessment presents a risk that the OA becomes viewed as bureaucratic and unnecessary, which would be undesirable.

To mitigate this risk, Edinburgh University Library sought to ensure that it was always presenting OA in a positive light, relaying important information about the benefits of OA to researchers, such as a likelihood of increased citations for research papers due to enhanced access. This was tempered with the pressing need to inform researchers about the urgency of taking action on OA in order to ensure that research outputs would be eligible for the REF. This could sometimes be problematic as words such as 'compliance' tend to be offputting and have unfortunate connotations of bureaucracy.

A further challenge is that some academics try to apply the OA requirements only to those research outputs they think they will be submitting to the next REF. In the last REF exercise, as in previous research assessment exercises, researchers have been asked to submit their four best papers from the assessment period (the last six or seven years).

There are several difficulties here: the researcher may not agree with colleagues over which papers are to be submitted, co-authors within the same institution may wish to submit the same paper, the University may have a different opinion than the author as to the quality of the output, the author may have unforeseen circumstances (meaning that they later need to rely on a paper previously not intended for inclusion), and finally, we do not know yet what the assessment requirements of the next REF will be. Perhaps all papers will need to be submitted. The policy was designed to cover all journal articles and conference proceedings, and so the best practice is to make sure that all papers meet the OA requirements so that they may be eligible for inclusion in the REF.

Perhaps the greatest challenge in implementing the REF OA policy is actually getting the academic culture to change. With appropriate resources in place, administration in the Schools or in the library can check repository submissions and make a paper OA, but the greatest challenge is to get the researcher to inform the repository administrator when something has been accepted for publication, because this is not part of current academic practice. Once this hurdle is overcome, the rest should be plain sailing.

Successes and best practice for open access implementation

The first achievement was to define a plan for implementing the REF OA requirements that was acceptable to the University and was approved by Research Policy Group. Gaining senior management buy-in for this work has been absolutely critical to its success, and will continue to be in the future.

The decentralized implementation model employed at Edinburgh has been incredibly helpful in getting recognition of the policy and buy-in from local research leads within different disciplines. These School-level Research Directors often have great influence over their colleagues and having them as local champions for the policy can be really useful. Furthermore, as OA is now a matter closely related to REF, these individuals have taken more personal responsibility for the performance of their Schools, which has helped to increase levels of compliance with the policy.

Top tips:

- Make sure University senior management are aware of the policy and its implications (bonus points for early adoption).
- Treat the implementation like a project, with defined timescales. Formulate a project plan and stick to it (plan your work and work your plan).
- Think about what staffing resources will be needed to manage the project, conduct advocacy, check repository records, provide reports, etc. If you don't have much scope for extra staff resources, is there any existing work you could stop doing?
- Provide clear, simple guidance for researchers.
- Review progress regularly and don't be afraid to make changes (regular reporting is helpful).
- Apply the same policy across the institution and don't be tempted to make exceptions for individual Schools or groups of researchers.

Supporting best practice across the UK

When a new policy such as this is announced, universities may not be prepared for proactive advocacy and timely compliance for many reasons; they may lack staff, knowledge or the financial resources. Given the wide scope and broad impact of research funders' OA policies, as well as the differing workflows and approaches of universities across the sector, examples are needed of effective practice that are collaboratively developed but reflect institutional difference within a 'real-world' environment.

Jisc has commissioned a portfolio of Open Access Pathfinder Projects aimed at helping reduce the fragmentation of practice and put in place mechanisms to capture and share lessons quickly and iteratively around the dynamic OA environment (Jisc, 2015).

The University of Edinburgh leads the LOCH Project (Lessons in Open Access Compliance for Higher Education), which is already providing guidance to other institutions on the implementation of both green and gold OA (University of Edinburgh, 2015b). The project has shared a wide variety of guidance materials to help staff in different universities plan for the implementation of the OA requirements for REF and to provide support and guidance to a range of stakeholders. Project outputs include implementation plans, checklists, text for web pages and a wealth of documentation to help practitioners in the UK with the considerable task ahead.

Conclusions

The UK has been engaged with the OA agenda for over a decade, but progress has undoubtedly been slow. Policies have been conflicting and early university and research funder policies on OA often lacked any sanctions for non-compliance, so were seen as 'toothless' by busy researchers.

The 2012 revision of the RCUK policy undoubtedly helped to increase awareness of OA, as well as increased deposits in institutional repositories and demand for gold OA funding. However, linking OA with research assessment has done more than anything else to get authors interested in and talking about OA.

It is of critical importance that we continue to convey an upbeat, positive message about the value of OA to authors during this time of transition. There is a real danger that authors lose sight of the good things that OA can do for them, and a risk that it becomes perceived as a pointless bureaucratic exercise. At the same time, researchers need to be made aware of the potentially serious consequences of not engaging with open access.

Universities in the UK are working hard to prepare for the REF requirements to 'go live' on 1 April 2016. There is much work to do, and many conversations to be had, but success with this new policy could prove to be a real milestone in the transition towards open access. Success could mean that the UK could be in a position where a vast majority of journal articles and conference proceedings are available on an open access basis.

References

European Commission (2015) *Horizon 2020 Open Access Policy*, http://ec.europa.eu/research/swafs/index.cfm?pg=policy&lib=science.

Higher Education Funding Council for England (HEFCE) (n.d.) *REF Open Access Requirements*, www.hefce.ac.uk/rsrch/oa/Policy/.

Jisc (n.d.). *Repositories Support Project*, www.rsp.ac.uk.

Jisc (2009) *EMBRACE (EMbedding Repositories And Consortial Enhancement) Project: final report*, http://discovery.ucl.ac.uk/14849/1/14849.pdf.

Jisc (2015) Pathfinder Projects, *Open Access Good Practice*, http://openaccess.jiscinvolve.org/wp/pathfinder-projects.

Research Councils UK (RCUK) (2014) *Open Access Policy*, www.rcuk.ac.uk/research/openaccess.

Tate, D. (2014) *RCUK Open Access Report 2014*, University of Edinburgh, www.era.lib.ed.ac.uk/handle/1842/9386.

University of Edinburgh (2015a) *Open Access Requirements in the Post-2014 REF Proposed Implementation Approach*, www.crc.hss.ed.ac.uk/docs/open/CRC_060515_01_Open_Access.pdf.

University of Edinburgh (2015b) *Lessons in Open Access Compliance for Higher Education (LOCH) Project*, http://libraryblogs.is.ed.ac.uk/loch.

Wellcome Trust (n.d.) *FP7 Open Access Policy: position statement in support of open and unrestricted access to published research*, www.wellcome.ac.uk/About-us/Policy/Policy-and-position-statements/WTD002766.htm.

CHAPTER 8

Bridging the gap: easing the transition to higher education with an information literacy MOOC

*Mariann Løkse, Helene N. Andreassen,
Torstein Låg and Mark Stenersen*

Introduction

What do students need to learn to get the most out of their academic studies? How can the library support their learning process in the best possible way? Are our current information literacy (IL) classes what we want them to be?

After repeatedly asking ourselves these questions, we gradually realized we needed to refocus and adjust our teaching and learning services to meet the needs of new students. Thus, the iKomp MOOC (Massive Open Online Course) was born, and with it a chance to introduce modern teaching methods in our IL instruction, together with a more dialogue-based communication with first-year students.

The main trigger for starting to change how we teach information literacy at our university came from feeling that we, in some respects, failed in reaching the students with our instruction. With the norm being one or two classes with each student group during their first term, we had a lot to say and sadly not enough time in which to say it. Our lectures were packed with all the wonderful stuff that we as librarians know could help the student's research and learning process. Feedback from attending students was usually very good, but what did they really learn? Moreover, what about those students who for some reason did not attend?

As we created a MOOC to address these challenges, another important factor dawned on us. Many of the students who tested the beta version of iKomp repeatedly mentioned the gap between secondary and higher education. Reflecting on this issue, we understood more clearly the importance of the library's learning support services. Young people enter universities and colleges with a varying set of expectations, learning skills and basic knowledge. Similarly, higher education faculty have their own expectations of their students. These two sets of expectations are not necessarily in agreement.

In this chapter, we describe the development of our MOOC, entitled iKomp and created at UiT, The Arctic University of Norway, in the period 2013–15 (http://ikomp.no). The chapter is organized as follows: first, we present iKomp and then we expand on the needs that caused us to develop it. The following section is devoted to the reasons we had for creating the course on a MOOC platform, and we go on to detail the platform selection and course implementation. In the next section we review the reception of iKomp, followed by a section presenting the lessons learned. We close our chapter in a final section with some reflections on how iKomp can support research and learning.

iKomp course description

iKomp is composed of four independent, yet interrelated, modules. These have been selected on the basis of our personal experience as IL teachers, as well as from discussions about which skills we, and the university in general, expect students to acquire, preferably during their first term. The modules are:

1   Learning Strategies
2   Information Evaluation
3   The Information Search Process
4   Academic Formation.

The main objective of the first module, Learning Strategies, is encouraging students to reflect on their own learning techniques. Taking an active role in what and how to learn, by planning, reading critically and testing ourselves while we read, is a key element of academic success. Many students struggle, however, with the independence and freedom of choice afforded to members of the academic community. In this regard, a clearly defined study plan can help many to improve their academic working habits and thus perform better at assignments and exams.

With masses of information being available to us all from a wide spectrum of channels, it is no wonder that being able to sort out academic texts from the rest is a challenge to students. In the second module, Information Evaluation, we discuss the importance of assessing and critically analysing the sources we use, which is a task many students have little experience in, since from primary and secondary school they are used to teachers telling them what to read and why.

Searching for literature is rarely considered a challenge, and this might be because we always find *something* when we search, no matter how poorly we perform. However, we often fail to assess whether this *something* is actually the best and most relevant search result. The third module of iKomp, The

Information Search Process, teaches students how to find relevant and quality-assured sources while minimizing the amount of noise in the search results.

The fourth and final module of iKomp, concentrating on the use of sources, is Academic Formation. The wording of the title is deliberate, as we want to focus on more than just citations and references. In addition to understanding why use of sources is essential to the academic enterprise, we want students to reflect on respect, integrity and honesty as key elements in academia, and on their own motivation for a university degree. We do, however, also take them through the dos and don'ts of citation techniques, given that this is a necessary student skill, and of concern to both faculty and students.

Each module contains a set of activities relating to the various topics presented in the texts and videos. For every activity, the learning objectives and the benefits of meeting these are clearly stated in an introductory text. The separate modules end with a formative quiz to help the students test if they have learned the basics. A 40-question multiple choice test, with questions based on the course content, rounds up the entire MOOC. After submitting the answers, an explanation is given for each question to explain why one alternative is considered better than the others. A score of 80% and above generates a course diploma, which in turn can be uploaded in the students' Learning Management System as proof of their passing the course.

iKomp as a response to the needs of IL instructors and students
Effective teaching with limited time

Academic librarians teaching information literacy often face dilemmas arising from the limited time typically allocated to this service. Usually, IL instruction is reduced to one or two brief sessions, sometimes even scheduled outside regular class meetings. Becoming information-literate is about academic skills and attitudes, as well as knowledge, and fitting all the necessary instruction into a few hours is simply not feasible – at least not if we want to teach effectively. We therefore need to prioritize. We need to decide what to leave out and to what extent we explain the whys and the hows. We further need to decide upon discussion v. practice, i.e. do we ask students to think about and discuss ways to evaluate and credit their sources, or do we instead guide them in searching for information or citing sources?

International research has shown that active learning approaches to instruction (e.g. classroom discussion, problem solving and formative testing) on average lead to better learning than traditional forms of teaching (e.g. lecturing or 'chalk and talk') (Freeman et al., 2014; Prince, 2004). Active learning, however, requires preparation by the students. Unguided or unstructured forms of active learning, such as 'pure' discovery learning, may be counterproductive (Kirschner, Sweller and Clark, 2006). When solving problems or discussing, on the other hand, students need to know which concepts to apply, and to have some idea of how to approach a certain type of problem. Nonetheless, when time is scarce, IL instructors often deliberately ignore the benefits of classroom activities, and limit themselves to the basics of 'traditional' information literacy, leaving the students to practise applying the material on their own. Guided and productive student activity in IL classroom sessions may yet be achievable, even with limited time. If IL instructors could introduce new concepts and go over a few examples outside class time, then we could devote in-class time to guided learning activities. This teaching model, known as the *flipped* or *inverted classroom* (Lage, Platt and Treglia, 2000; Sams and Bergmann, 2012), does, however, require suitable online learning materials. iKomp was designed to meet this requirement.

Helping students see the big picture

Learning well is hard work. Moreover, trying to learn something when we cannot see the point of doing so is boring, even gruelling, and very likely to fail. To a new student, learning the intricate details of finding and citing sources often feels time-consuming, and in the end, rather meaningless. Citations and references, for instance, can by many students be perceived as quite hard to grasp. Whatever they already know about this topic from secondary education is usually not enough to satisfy the requirements of a university-level assignment. Students rapidly realize they need to get these things right somehow, because their teachers require it. Yet, they often see these requirements as just a silly formality, as part of the 'academic game' they need to play to pass and earn their grade. Consequently, if they can satisfy the requirements without spending too much effort, i.e. without actually learning how and why they should cite sources, they will.

As IL instructors, we traditionally tend to spend too much of our classroom sessions on the details of citing literature. Of course, helping students get it right may be worthwhile in and of itself, but unless they abstract more *general* knowledge from learning about citation techniques, they are likely to need help with it again later. Thus, through years of evaluation of our own in-class sessions, we now see a clear need to step away from the details of citations and literature searches, and to deal with the reasons why these skills are relevant for learning. iKomp has allowed us to relocate training on searching and citing to the online environment, and thereby devote face-to-face meetings entirely to issues we consider far more important, i.e. how information literacy skills can foster learning.

Why choose a MOOC to teach IL?
Reaching all students

The last decades have seen notable changes in higher education. While institutions experience more competition and economic pressure, student enrolment and diversity have increased in both Europe and the USA. This, in turn, has altered student behaviour, to which we must relate. An increasing number of students study part-time or attend flexible education programmes, and spend very little time on campus. As for current on-campus students, their presence in the classroom varies highly in courses with optional attendance. Moreover, when we take into account that many of today's students tend to mainly focus on tasks explicitly transmittable to exam preparations, courses provided by the library are low on their list of priorities. Furthermore, the students who actually turn up to IL sessions are not necessarily the ones most in need of information literacy teaching.

When taking into account the array of practical and pedagogical factors we wanted to improve in our instruction services, we decided to create a MOOC, or Massive Open Online Course. This resource was designed as a freestanding service to all students, including the many off-campus students, and can function as a substitute for, or as a supplement to, our on-campus instruction.

Encouraging student engagement

A central role of university libraries is to support teaching and learning, and we therefore need to adapt to changes in higher education. Not only should we strive to reach all students, but we should also aim to enhance student learning by opting for a more agile teaching methodology.

Creating iKomp has enabled us to actively approach this goal. We have changed our on-campus instruction by introducing a partly flipped classroom method, increased our use of student response systems, and focused more on student participation. By asking the students to do all or part of the MOOC in advance, they come prepared and we can devote our lessons to discussion and activities concerning the more important information literacy topics.

By making students reflect on the bigger issues in iKomp prior to attending an IL lesson, they more easily relate to the content and see the relevance to their own studies. *Activity and motivation* is the key combination for the students to engage (see Barkley, 2010), which in turn is a prerequisite for learning well. Implementing our MOOC has thus had a wider and more positive effect on our instruction services than originally planned.

Developing an IL course on a MOOC platform

When we set out to create iKomp, we decided to make it available to as many as possible. The idea of making a MOOC was always our intention, but it did pose some challenges for the course development team. The 'M' in MOOC refers to 'massive', as in a large mass of students, and also 'massive' as in the scalability of the platform. Finding the right platform turned out to be of the utmost importance.

Apart from having a good idea and a good concept for a course, defining the learning outcomes was high on the priority list; obvious with regard to the actual course contents, but just as crucial when planning the necessary technical properties. Both script team and designer needed to know how the course should look and feel, and how participants should interact with the contents.

Choosing a platform

We started out with a list of some possible platforms, each with different qualities. As mentioned above, the learning outcomes defined for the course were central for the selection of types of instruction and activities in iKomp, and therefore key to choosing the right platform. MOOCs usually make extensive use of videos, together with interactive elements such as exercises, multiple-choice tests or other activities. Given this variety of pedagogical tools, only when having a clear idea of the content and ways of interacting with students were we able decide on which platform to use.

For the iKomp course we decided to use the OpenEdX platform, a platform designed entirely with course development in mind. Our main reason for using OpenEdX was its simplicity in user interaction design, ease of use for script teams, and its structural and linear course design.

Course types and contents

Online courses are usually built in one of two ways: linear or non-linear. In non-linear design, students are guided through the contents by instruction (e.g. 'After watching the video, go to the corresponding course notes'). By contrast, participants in a linear course always know where they are, and the system keeps track of which chapters and sections they have completed.

After careful consideration of our course contents, we decided on technologies and designs that we thought would work best for our intended audience. iKomp was therefore designed to activate users through the use of videos, texts, activities and tests, and the overall graphic design had to be visually pleasing and interesting. Repeatedly revisiting our intended learning outcomes was crucial to the coherence of the end result.

Combining your contents

During a visit to the University of Alberta, we found that in their newest production, Onlea's VP Production, Kevin Barrett, promoted a rigid course design, which first presents 90 seconds of video, then an interactive object (e.g. an animation or multiple choice questions). This design becomes quite repetitive, being consistently implemented throughout the course. Although this method of online course design has comprehensive research behind it, it does not necessarily work in all circumstances. In light of our own experience, we would therefore advise you to trust your own instincts regarding how you combine your contents. There are no rules, but we recommend that you test the course on someone similar to the target audience to ensure its effectiveness.

iKomp was originally planned as a linear course. This model provided us with an opportunity to guide the learner through an experience that was designed to build on previous learning, which, in turn, gave the course a sense of direction. However, our course design team was also devoted to open content, freely available to anyone at any time. Combining a linear and non-linear model removed some limiting restrictions, creating a course that not only takes the user on a guided journey towards a course certificate, but that also works as an open resource throughout the course of study.

Research opportunities

MOOCs presently receive much attention as a research area. If you choose the OpenEdX platform, everything the participants do is collected and stored as event data in a module called *Insights*. If you do not intend to carry out research on your MOOC, the data is still of great value to many other researchers. We advise you to be part of the open source community and share.

The reception of iKomp

Throughout the project period, we have emphasized evaluation of the course composition and content. As our over-arching perspective was to meet students' needs, we hired two students to provide feedback on the first version of iKomp. To capture the variations between different disciplines, we selected one student enrolled in a regulated three-year study programme in the health sciences, and another student enrolled in a more flexible study programme in the humanities. While their oral and written feedback confirmed that we were on the right track, they also suggested adjustments to the activities, the texts and the order of the modules. Additionally, we realized that both activities and videos were easily disregarded when time is scarce. To reduce the risk of skipping useful parts, we made sure to repeatedly and explicitly underline the deeper reasons why students should devote time to the various components.

Further, to ensure that the course content was in line with our overall intentions, we collaborated with five departments at our university, and invited their students to test the beta version of iKomp. The invitation stressed the importance of their feedback, and to encourage written evaluation, we advertised a raffle in which the winner would receive a tablet. Discussions with faculty and administrative staff during the beta testing revealed unconditional enthusiasm. They clearly saw the need for this type of course, and they were interested in and appreciated the approach taken, with its focus on the broader aspects of academic life. Several departments expressed interest in integrating the final version of iKomp as an obligatory part of the curriculum.

Before officially releasing iKomp, we sent an open invitation to our library colleagues to take the course and provide us with feedback. While this enabled us to make final adjustments, it also introduced iKomp to all corners of our organization, thereby instigating a sense of ownership, crucial for future promotion to students and employees.

Lessons learned

A MOOC is not built in a day, nor even in a few months, unless you have unlimited resources at your disposal. Our group has spent more time on the iKomp project than any of us could have foreseen. Although our workload has varied according to the various stages of development, from start to finish, six people at the university library have spent almost two years developing the course.

Do not let this discourage you, however. We do not regret for one second spending so much time creating our online resource. We have gained insight regarding information literacy, teaching and technology, but more importantly, we have provided all students at our university with an information literacy course – available whenever they need it. Further, the project has increased the visibility of the library's teaching and learning services to both faculty and university administration.

One major benefit of project-based course development is the fruits of increased co-operation between different sections of the library. Looking back, we are convinced that three aspects have been key to the final product:

1　Combining various competencies and experiences
2　A common goal
3　A determination to spend long hours, not all of them sunny and bright, to reach this goal.

Good co-operation means honest feedback from fellow project members, from content details to main objectives, from spelling errors to selection of technical solutions. Being able, as a group, to extract the essentials of information literacy as well as how to teach it, we see the final course content as adaptable to every level in every study programme.

Before concluding this chapter, we present the factors we consider most important in the development of iKomp.

People

Choosing the right people to work with proved to be a most significant decision. Developing a new learning resource requires competencies in areas like education, graphic design and information literacy. Equally important is high work ethics, and not the least, the social skills necessary to make the group work.

The process included several work-intensive periods with long hours and some tedious rounds of editing and evaluation. It was crucial for the finished product that the members of our group worked well together and were able to have fun in the midst of it all.

Our tip: Choose people with different strengths, who will work well together. Someone with a grasp of design and/or technology will be invaluable.

Funding

Libraries rarely have sufficient budgets to allow members of staff to lay aside their ordinary work to concentrate on specific tasks over a certain period. All six of us worked with iKomp in addition to doing our full-time jobs at the library. Since everything we did (in theory) was done within our working hours, extra funding was not strictly necessary. In addition, we chose the open-source platform OpenEdX, thus avoiding the cost of expensive software. We did however apply for – and received – two small grants, which made it possible for activities such as travelling to conferences and having the course translated into English.

Our tip: Extra funding is a welcome bonus, but if it is not possible, do not let it stop you.

Planning

We spent a few months planning and deciding on which elements to include in the course. This first period felt quite slow, and we were not too sure where we were heading. Then, we were fortunate to get a meeting with plagiarism expert Jude Carroll, and discussed the different aspects of information literacy with her. Meeting with someone from 'the outside' who provided guidance on which direction to take proved extremely helpful.

Furthermore, receiving extra funding enabled us to leave town and spend a couple of days in a cottage with the specific purpose of deciding on a project plan and a course structure. This workshop in unfamiliar surroundings helped us concentrate on the work ahead and ultimately proved successful. After that, the ball really started rolling.

Our tip: Plan properly – it will save you time!

Writing and creating content

After our kick-off workshop, the challenging work of creating content began. Four of us concentrated on the writing, with continuous feedback from the rest of the group. Ideas on activities were thoroughly discussed in the group before being developed. It took around eight months to have a product ready for beta testing. Multiple writers on a project can be a challenge, but if the writing styles are not too diverse it is usually helpful to share the work.

Our tip: Creating good and relevant activities takes far more time than writing texts, so concentrate on those.

Testing and student feedback

From the start, we had a strong ambition to make an online course that students could both like and learn from. To ensure we did not create a course that only librarians would love (it has been known to happen), we asked for student feedback throughout.

In our experience, you can only get so far on your own. Having students working on the course and commenting on content is invaluable. In our case, this led to much improvement, for instance, creating more activities and providing additional examples.

Our tip: Get feedback from your target groups, even if it costs you an iPad.

Revision

Testing has no effect if the results are not used to enhance your product. You must therefore expect to spend some time revising and editing. Based on the valuable feedback we got from students, we sat down, rewrote and further adjusted the course. In addition, our graphic designer did a marvellous job on the visuals of the course. He was also our tech guru, and sorted out things that did not work well enough in the beta version.

Our tip: Take the feedback seriously and revise your course accordingly. Pay attention to the graphic design.

Launch and promotion

Promoting library services to the university community is certainly an area with which we struggle. We should use all the information channels we have access to, including social media, websites, meetings, e-mails, etc. Talks with teachers and departments are ongoing, and we will have to continue ensuring that students actually find iKomp useful. We still have a way to go before reaching our goal of enough people knowing about iKomp to justify the 'M' in MOOC.

Our tip: Never overestimate what your patrons know about the library. There will always be some groups that need more information about your products and services.

Conclusion: how does iKomp support research and learning?

What is the point of a university? Why are we here? Why are the students here? These questions may seem naïve, but we think they are too seldom asked and rarely answered. Still, most people in academia will agree that these questions are quite important and in fact touch upon the very notion of academic practice. There is a specific reason for our obsession with these big questions, though, and that is that they are connected to other questions – questions that a new student might ask herself: 'Should I bother looking for another source?' 'Why is my professor so obsessed with the details of my reference list?' 'Could I just borrow some of these sentences for my own paper?' An information-literate student should be able to answer these latter questions for herself, or at least choose a sensible course of action. However, as academic librarians are well aware of, helping students become information-literate is no easy task. The reasons for this are numerous, but two stand out as particularly challenging:

1   IL instructors often meet only briefly with students in one or two sessions.
2   Students may have conceptions about learning, knowledge and higher education that make them less likely to see the connection between IL and their chosen discipline.

iKomp tries to address these two points by being a resource available to students 24/7 and by emphasizing skills that are valued in all academic settings.

The ultimate aim of the course is to enhance the students' learning experience. Mastering some basic learning techniques can have a great impact on a student's perception of mastering her studies. Furthermore, by making students reflect on searching for, evaluating and using literature, we are training them in the academic research process, and consequently increasing their understanding of what research is and how it can be used in academia and in society in general.

Looking back, iKomp was a natural course of development for IL pedagogy in our library. New elements have been added and old elements have been refined; we have made information literacy training accessible to anyone; and faculty can refer to the course instead of spending valuable classroom time explaining academic integrity and citation techniques. Students can use the course as an introduction to what is expected of them in higher education, or as a helpful tool when they are writing – wherever they are and whenever they need it.

For us as IL instructors at the University Library, the development and launch of iKomp has merely been the first, albeit the largest, step in an ongoing process of improving library services. The next step is to continue promoting the course to optimize its use – at UiT and elsewhere. Moreover, a MOOC needs to be regularly reviewed and updated to make sure it stays relevant to its users. Finally, an important task ahead is to determine whether iKomp actually has any effect on student learning. Given the Insights module inherent in the OpenEdX platform, we can analyse user data in a deeper fashion than in any other teaching and learning service we provide at the library.

It is our belief that the kind of data MOOCs and other online courses can provide to research communities will impact both teaching and learning in the near future. As for iKomp and our own library, we strongly believe that delving into the user data will help us better understand the students, thereby enabling us to modify our teaching and learning services (in-class, blended or online), and consequently strengthening the modern university library's supporting role in higher education. If our MOOC can help prepare students for the expectations of academia and guide them towards being independent learners and critical thinkers, this will improve their overall student experience, their academic skills, and ultimately their understanding of their chosen discipline.

References

Barkley, E. F. (2010) *Student Engagement Techniques: a handbook for college faculty*, San Francisco, CA, Jossey-Bass.

Freeman, S., Eddy, S. L., McDonough, M., Smith, M. K., Okoroafor, N., Jordt, H. and Wenderoth, M. P. (2014) Active Learning Increases Student Performance in Science, Engineering and Mathematics, *Proceedings of the National Academy of Sciences*, **111** (23), 8410–15, DOI: 10.1073/pnas.1319030111.

Kirschner, P. A., Sweller, J. and Clark, R. E. (2006) Why Minimal Guidance During Instruction Does Not Work: an analysis of the failure of constructivist, discovery, problem-based, experiential, and inquiry-based teaching, *Educational Psychologist*, **41** (2), 75–86, DOI: 10.1207/s15326985ep4102_1.

Lage, M. J., Platt, G. J. and Treglia, M. (2000) Inverting the Classroom: a gateway to creating an inclusive learning environment, *Journal of Economic Education*, **31** (1), 30–43.

Prince, M. (2004) Does Active Learning Work?: a review of the research, *Journal of Engineering Education*, **93** (3), 223–31.

Sams, A. and Bergmann, J. (2012) *Flip Your Classroom: reach every student in every class every day*, Eugene, OR, International Society for Technology in Education.

CHAPTER 9

Metadata enhancement through name authority in the UNT Digital Library

Hannah Tarver and Mark Phillips

Introduction

Historically, libraries have focused not only on building collections, but on creating a means of describing these resources to make them discoverable and useful. Over time, cataloguing – or, more broadly, metadata creation – has been standardized in various structured ways to ensure consistency at a local level and the ability to easily share resource descriptions among institutions. Within these structures, authority control functions as a key component for usability by enabling optimal search and retrieval of relevant resources by users. Simply defined, authority control is the process of identifying a single preferred or 'authorized' format of a value that should be used in place of alternative spellings or synonyms to create consistent entries. There are a number of areas in which authority control is important for libraries, including subjects, locations and names of organizations, events and persons.

Name authority tends to pose a particular problem, because a metadata creator may need additional information associated with an authority heading to determine whether a name applies (particularly in the case of multiple persons with similar names). This may require a separate database of authority entries with contextual information, rather than a list of authorized terms or thesaurus, which are sufficient for some forms of authority control. Tillett (1989) notes that authority work generally involves research of names as well as documenting information in a name authority file such as 'the authority data of preferred form, variants, history, scope, and links to other authority records.' A number of initiatives in the library environment, both historically and in the present, have attempted to generate and share name authority records, and to address the challenge of keeping these systems up to date and relevant. Typically national libraries throughout the world take responsibility for names that are important to their national domain, including authors and organizations from their country that create resources of interest to their users. In the USA, this work has been carried out for decades by the Library of Congress (LOC) with their Name Authority File (LCNAF).[1] Containing over eight million records, this dataset comprises names of people and organizations that appear in the LOC catalogue.

In the past decade there has been an asserted effort to move name authority files from locally managed library databases to the open web. For example, Ilik (2014) discusses the growing need to incorporate name authority sources and tools beyond traditional MARC records to better serve local needs. The goal is to make use of technologies such as linked open data (LOD) in order to capitalize on the extensive name authority work we've already done in this space, so that it becomes more widely adoptable and usable by the rest of the web. The Library of Congress id.loc.gov system makes available a number of controlled vocabularies and name authority files as linked open data, which represents a major step toward open, shareable authority information in the USA. The Virtual International Authority File (VIAF)[2] from OCLC furthers this work by aggregating name authority files from more than 24 national libraries and many other organizations around the world, matching name concepts that are the same, and making them available as linked data with established relationships between the different representations of the same entity (OCLC, 2015). VIAF has successfully generated and exposed LOD, and has been used on the web to help populate Wikipedia with name authority information (OCLC, 2012a). In the library sphere, VIAF has contributed to the work OCLC has done on its WorldCat product, which now provides millions of bibliographic records that are using the schema.org vocabularies (OCLC, 2012b).

Academic names

While these efforts represent a massive amount of work, communication, negotiation and finally agreement, they do not represent the full needs of academic institutions to manage identification of names within our systems. In 2009, Salo pointed out some of the difficulties in maintaining name authority in institutional repositories due to the varying sources of metadata, limitations of the systems and specificity of name authority systems. Many of the systems mentioned above are primarily populated with names and identities of notable people throughout history, politicians, performers, authors and artists. Furthermore, the authors represented in traditional name authority files tend to be solely those who have written books, rather than representing the wider array of scholarly publishing. No one organization can manage name authority files for all entities that might need to be represented in metadata records; however, this means that large, established name authority files are suboptimal for managing the wide range of resources held at academic institutions. In particular, institutions that want to manage the scholarly research output of their faculty and staff may have difficulty managing names for persons who primarily publish scholarly or scientific articles, for which even widely published authors may never receive a LCNAF record, nor make their way into VIAF.

In 2013 the University of North Texas (UNT) Libraries demonstrated this phenomenon with research into the number of instances of name authority records that existed in local bibliographic records, VIAF, LCNAF, or in Wikipedia for 100 randomly selected authors who had materials in the UNT Scholarly Works collection (UNT's institutional repository). This data is presented in Table 9.1.

Table 9.1 *VIAF, LOC and Wikipedia name authority record comparison (Tarver et al., 2013)*	
UNT Scholarly Works Repository	100 (random sampling)
Local bibliographic records	26
VIAF records	32
LCNAF records	28
Wikipedia	2

As evidenced by the data, only 26% of names are found in the local bibliographic records, 32% have an authority file in the VIAF database, 28% have an authority file in the LCNAF and only 2% of names were found in Wikipedia. Additionally, most authors with a record in one authority control file overlap with those controlled in another; therefore, the total number of authors represented in all of these authority files is still roughly one-third of the total authors in the random sample. To control names for the full scope of resources in an academic library, we need a different approach to bridge this gap.

In the late 2000s a number of initiatives set out to help with this problem, such as Open Researcher and Contributor ID (ORCID)[3] and International Standard Name Identifier (ISNI),[4] which were created to help facilitate the creation of unique identifiers for all interested authors in the academic publication space. This work has been successful, with over 1.3 million unique author identifiers being created in the ORCID system by 2015. These provide yet another source of identifiers and another tool for authority control (by using the identifier as the representation of the name in a linked data context) to manage names in the academic environment. Institutions such as Texas A&M have begun the process of registering masters- and doctoral-level students with ORCID in order to establish unique identifiers for the students that they can use throughout their careers (Texas A&M University Libraries, 2015). Additionally, many granting institutions and publishers now allow for primary investigators and authors to submit ORCIDs in addition to their names so that there is no question about which 'John Smith' is publishing a paper or submitting a grant.

With all of these opportunities for names, one might think that there is a goldmine for metadata creators and system designers in the academic library context; however, great abundance does not eliminate all challenges. One challenge is the need to establish names for authors who are no longer living, but who were never assigned an authority record in a traditional or more recent system. Additionally, with millions of name authority records available, it is now possible to further confuse a metadata creator or end-user by incorrectly selecting a record that appears correct but which might point to a different person with a similar name. A contrived example of this would be if there were two authors named Jane Smith who were publishing at the same time in similar-sounding fields, say linguistics and computational linguistics. With even more authority files in a variety of places, it is possible that having more authors named 'Jane Smith' as options for metadata creation could create additional confusion. For instance, at the time of writing there are 3 ORCIDs for persons named Mark Phillips; however, 0000-0002-9679-6730 is the identifier for the Mark Phillips involved in the writing of this chapter.

While there is no single, perfect answer, we decided that the best option at UNT would be a locally built name authority system which would let us manage locally important names and also leverage existing name authority tools such as Wikipedia, ORCID, VIAF and LCNAF. This provides us the ability to improve not only the metadata creation process within academic libraries but also to improve the users' experiences with our systems.

Background

The UNT Libraries have been acquiring and hosting digital materials for more than ten years. Although all of the items reside in the same digital library infrastructure, they are searchable by end-users through three separate interfaces: The Portal to Texas History,[5] the UNT Digital Library,[6] and The Gateway to Oklahoma History.[7] Over the years, we have recognized the importance of metadata in our digital collections and the potential for leveraging metadata values to support user interfaces and functionality. For example, when users search in one of the interfaces, the system automatically generates browsable facets based on values in several of our metadata fields, including resource type, coverage place and language. Within individual records many values, such as names, locations and subjects, become clickable links that launch a search in our system for other items with the same value.

However, this dependence on metadata values requires a relatively high level of consistency across collections. All of the items in our collections are described using a locally modified Dublin Core schema containing 21 available fields. Whenever possible, field values – and all qualifiers – are limited to controlled vocabulary options. Our vocabularies (UNT Vocabularies[8]) are maintained as RDF-compliant open linked data, which is connected to our metadata system so that vocabularies display as drop-down menus. Additionally, we have extensive documentation detailing how metadata creators should format and enter information in each metadata field, with examples and resources (University of North Texas Libraries, 2015).

In terms of name authority, we have controlled names informally by encouraging the use of established authority records (including LCNAF and VIAF) when relevant. For names without authority records, we suggested general formatting guidelines, such as inverting personal names, using the fullest form of the name available (James rather than J.) and removing prefixes and suffixes except those necessary to identify an individual. We also attempted to use consistent formatting of each name within a collection of items. Although this helped to create general consistency within our records, there was still a need for more formal authority control, particularly within collections containing names associated with UNT. Many of the collections hosted in our system are owned and managed by partner institutions, and so the amount of contextual information that we have for metadata or authority control is limited; however, names associated with UNT fall within the direct domain of our institution and are unlikely to be controlled by any other entity. It was still not always possible to find the most appropriate version of a name, or to verify that two similar names (e.g., Smith, D. and Smith, Don) were in fact the same person. These factors, in part, led to the development of the UNT Name App.[9]

UNT Name App

The UNT Name App is a web-based application designed to allow us to locally manage name authority within our system. We had several goals, which included: making our work compatible with other name authority initiatives around the library world, working within the existing structures and best practices of linked open data (LOD) and putting something in place that would require little work while still delivering a service that was usable in our local digital library system. To that end we decided to build a Django-based application written in Python that would act as both a website for our name authority service and as a set of application programming interfaces (APIs) that we could use in our digital library infrastructure.

We had several design goals in mind while building this tool. First, we decided that we wanted to map our work into the Metadata Authority Description Schema (MADS) standard.[10] The Library of Congress used this vocabulary as the successor to MARC-based name authority records. However, we also wanted to work directly within the greater LOD community, so we used the core components of MADS as the primary data model and extended it to allow us to represent relationships with other existing identifiers around the web (see Table 9.2).

Table 9.2 *Fields used in UNT Name App authority records*

Field	Required	Repeatable	Example	Notes
Name ID	Yes	No	nm0004212	Created by the system
Authoritative Name	Yes	No	Douglass, Neal	
Normalized Name	Yes	No	douglass neal	Machine generated by the system, using NACO transformation
Name Type	Yes	No	Personal	Options are Personal, Organization, Event, Software, Building
Biography/History	No	No	*May 15, 1988:* Name changed to University of North Texas	Text is formatted in Markdown with schema.org additions
Begin Date	No	No	1900-04-14	Extended Date/Time Format (EDTF)
End Date	No	No	1983-11-25	EDTF
Disambiguation	No	No	Photographer	
Record Status	Yes	No	Active	Options are Active, Deleted, Suppressed
Merged With	No	No		Used to merge two records for the same entity
Variant Name	No	Yes	UNT	Qualifier options are Acronym, Abbreviation, Translation, Expansion, Other
Identifier	No	Yes	http://viaf.org/viaf/125477573	Qualifier options include ORCID, VIAF, LCNAF, Wikipedia Link, Google Scholar, Citations Link, Homepage
Note	No	Yes		Qualifier options are Biographical/Historical, Deletion Information, Non-Public, Source, Other
Location	No	Yes	33.206537000-97.1727100000	Qualifier options are Current Location, Former Location

In addition to the support for a subset of MADS, we were interested in supporting the Schema.org[11] vocabularies. These vocabularies have become one of the primary ways institutions are sharing linked data, by marking up existing human-readable HTML-based web pages with machine-readable tags; this allows the same content to be a part of both the LOD community and the greater Semantic Web. Finally, we wanted a system that we could use for a variety of name types including people, organizations, pieces of software, events and finally buildings. This flexibility would allow us to use the same system and framework for a wide variety of names that needed to be locally defined.

As we were developing this system we had in mind the five stars of open linked data that Tim Berners-Lee enumerated in 2006:

- Make your stuff available on the web (whatever format) under an open licence.
- Make it available as structured data (e.g., Excel instead of an image scan of a table).
- Use non-proprietary formats (e.g., CSV instead of Excel).
- Use URIs to denote things, so that people can point at your stuff.
- Link your data to other data to provide context.

With an attempt to extend this five-star approach, we decided that there were actually four steps that we would follow for establishing name authority in a staged approach:

1 Put vocabularies on the web as five-star open linked data.
2 Make vocabularies available to metadata creators who actively use them.
3 Store links, not strings.
4 Make data meaningful to users.

Stage one: building the app

In order to have a reasonable, long-term solution, the first step was to create a system for name authority that would meet all of the requirements of the five stars of open linked data. The system would need to accommodate names with descriptions as well as representations of relationships between an established name, our locally created URI for the name and other web-based identifiers for the same entity. Additionally, we needed the ability to make this content available under a licence that allowed for – and encouraged – re-use and incorporation into other systems; without any chance of linking back into our authorities, our system would most likely not succeed.

We decided to represent our local data model in a number of machine-readable formats including a native JavaScript Object Notation (JSON)-based representation, a record-based format using the MADS schema, and a version of the data using the Schema.org vocabulary and inline micro-data mark-up. Each name in the UNT Name App would have a unique identifier, used to globally identify a specific name from other names that might be similar. Finally, we made sure to incorporate mechanisms for the establishment of relationships between our locally defined name authority record and other identifiers for the same name in other systems such as the Virtual International Authority File (VIAF), the Library of Congress Name Authority file (LCNAF) and web systems such as Wikipedia, Twitter and Google Scholar Citations,[12] among others (see Figure 9.1). These components together meet the requirements of five-star data by putting information on the web in a structured format (stars 1–3), assigning URIs (star 4) and linking to other systems for context (star 5).

> ★ Make your stuff available on the Web (whatever format) under an open licence
> ★ ★ Make it available as structured data (e.g., Excel instead of image scan of a table)
> ★ ★ ★ Use non-proprietary formats (e.g., CSV instead of Excel)
> ★ ★ ★ ★ Use URIs to denote things, so that people can point at your stuff
> ★ ★ ★ ★ ★ Link your data to other data to provide context

Figure 9.1 Example record in the UNT Name App

Stage two: making it available to metadata creators

Another important internal goal involved connecting the name authority files to the metadata creation process. Although the Name App was built in a way to make authority files and information externally visible and shareable, making tools available to metadata creators to incorporate name authority helps to ensure the use of established names. If metadata creators had to open a separate application to search for names, it would be harder to encourage continued authority control.

This stage was meant to provide a logical and straightforward way of allowing our metadata creators to insert name authority into their daily workflow. We accomplished this by creating a JSON web service or application-programming interface (API) in the UNT Name App that would allow remote systems to easily query and use authorized values or even the links themselves. Then we updated our metadata system so that our metadata entry form would query the Name App any time an editor started to type within a designated name field (for creators, contributors or publishers) and display possible matches (see Figure 9.2).

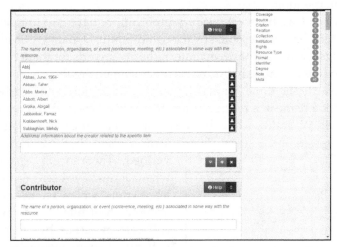

Figure 9.2 *Example type-ahead options in the metadata editing system*

Stage three: storing links

The next stage, storing links, will require a significant change to the underlying infrastructure that we have not yet made. However, the goal is to embed machine-readable URIs in the metadata stored by the system while displaying human-readable names for users. This change is necessary because computers can read and compare strings, but they cannot distinguish whether variations are all forms of the same name or different persons with similar names. As collections grow, there is an even greater chance that common or popular names will recur.

For example, we found a number of versions of the name Donald W. Smith (Don Smith, Donald Smith, Don W. Smith, etc.). A computer can easily compare these names and provide a probability that the names should all be the same; however, it cannot verify that the names all belong to the same person, or necessarily choose the most appropriate 'authorized' version – which may even be different from the available combinations. In fact, the name entries are spread across two different collections, including reports published by the National Advisory Committee for Aeronautics (NACA) during the 1940s–1950s and UNT theses and dissertations from the 2000s. Since the UNT professor listed as a committee member on the ETDs was still completing his bachelor's degree around the time that the NACA reports were published, we can make an educated assumption that there are probably two

Donald W. Smiths represented in our system: one who authored aeronautical engineering reports, and a UNT biology professor. However, we reached this conclusion by considering multiple contextual factors that generally require human intervention.

At this point we have a secondary problem; we have two unique persons in our system, both represented by the name 'Smith, Donald W.' So long as we store strings, even if we have separate authority records for these two people, there is no way to denote in the record *which* Donald Smith we mean – the text value is exactly the same. Similarly, there is no way for us to clearly express the fact that a name in a particular record has been verified and refers to 'the first' Donald W. Smith, while the same name in another record *might* be the same person, but has not yet been verified. Theoretically, storing links when names have been verified would let us note which names have been actively controlled and eventually collocate materials by an individual without retrieving materials by another author with the same name.

Another potential benefit is the possibility of enabling functionality to connect all items by an author while displaying different forms of a name.

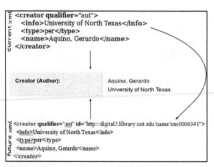

Figure 9.3 *Example of metadata with name identifier links in the XML coding*

For example, if we had a situation where we particularly wanted or needed to display the name as it appears on the item, we could store the link identifying the author to the system while displaying alternate text to users (see Figure 9.3).

The figure above contains an example (at the top) of the current XML coding used in the UNT Digital Library for a creator in which the name and information/affiliation are stored as strings. Simple controlled vocabularies represent creator type (person) and role (author) and show up as codes in the XML. Beneath, a snippet of modified XML illustrates metadata with a unique URL identifier associated with that name stored in the coding. How the name displays to the user may not change – shown in the centre of the figure – but the name could be displayed differently for different publications (e.g., as it appears on each item) while designating all records with the same URL name identifier as having the same creator or contributor.

Stage four: making names meaningful for users

Ultimately, a primary goal of linked data and projects that make use of various kinds of metadata is to create a system or interface that is more meaningful for users. When information is linked, it provides options to explain context, improve search options and create dynamic displays. In the commercial domain, companies have leveraged their resources to build specialized user interfaces around name authority, such as the Amazon author and artist pages,[13] WorldCat Identities[14] or Open Library author pages.[15] These pages help users find information about particular resources, but also provide contextual information, which may include biographical information, publishing or recording history, or recommendations for finding similar items.

Unfortunately, local institutional repositories (IRs) do not generally have the resources or large data stores to create similar systems. However, the names controlled in academic IRs and similar institutions are often not managed or well represented outside these organizations. This makes it even more important to expose name authority data and start building metadata that could be used to generate end-user functionality around academic names and names not represented in the commercial world.

Implementation

Once the Name App was built, we wanted to start compiling name authority records for entities in our system, even though the infrastructure and display pieces were ongoing. Until this point, names for scholarly materials had been entered in metadata records based on the version found on the item, since we did not have an efficient way of performing authority control. However, this led to retrieval issues that affected our campus and the wider research community using our items. Based on our primary goal of controlling institutionally important names, we started with names in the UNT Scholarly Works collection and our collection of UNT theses and dissertations.

Background on the collections

UNT started requiring graduate students to submit digital copies of theses and dissertations in 1999, meaning that more than ten years of modern electronic theses and dissertations (ETDs) are available in the UNT Digital Library. For this collection, author names are unlikely to create discrepancies, since most write only one thesis or dissertation; however, for each ETD we also document the student's committee members who signed off the thesis or dissertation. Professors may serve on many different committees over time and their names are often represented in different ways, depending on how a student submits them. For example the professor Dr William Moen may be referred to as Dr Moen, Bill Moen, Dr Bill Moen, Dr William Moen, or in an extreme case, Dr Bill. Additionally, we have been actively working to scan and provide access to UNT theses and dissertations published in print, prior to 1999, creating an even larger pool of names and variations. In the case of current professors, there is also the likelihood that some of the names will have crossover between this collection and UNT Scholarly Works.

In 2010 the UNT Libraries decided to develop an institutional repository for the scholarly output of the faculty, staff and students at UNT. While institutional repositories were in no sense a novel idea, this represented the first time that the UNT Libraries would make an overt effort to solicit, collect and provide access to these materials. The IR would also assist in fulfilling the expectations of the UNT Open Access Policy[16] passed by the UNT Faculty Senate and accepted by the UNT Regents as an official UNT Policy, encouraging UNT faculty and staff to deposit scholarly output. In practice, the UNT Scholarly Works IR is a collection within the greater UNT Digital Library.

Although staff members recognized the need for authority control within the IR, this was not a priority at the start of the collection, both because we did not have established mechanisms, and because there was a desire to show a quick amount of progress to demonstrate that the service was working as designed. This meant that authors' names might be entered under several variants if the versions of their names differed across publications, e.g., 'Laura Waugh' and 'L. Waugh.' By having two values for one name, end-users (often the authors themselves) might not be able to retrieve all of the expected publications written by a particular person.

Establishing name authority

In 2013 the UNT Name App had been built and we had identified the pilot collections. As a test, we extracted all creator and contributor names from the UNT Scholarly Works and ETD collections. These names and their associated name types (either person or organization) were compiled into a list, sorted and simplified by removing duplicate values. After that we used the UNT Name App's ingest API to establish new authority records for each of the names on the list.

At this point, staff members spent time identifying and merging records that represented the same identity. As records in the UNT Name App were merged, the metadata values for associated resources in the UNT Digital Library were also corrected manually, to match the authorized form of the name. When we finished with this set of names (over 3000 in total) we considered the data 'cleaned' and we were then able to run reports. This also let us experiment with new ways of interacting with the data that we were previously unable to do because of the inconsistency of the data in the system.

Today when we receive new resources for either the UNT Scholarly Works repository or the UNT Theses and Dissertations collection we add the names to the UNT Name App to establish them in the system before we create the bibliographic metadata for the item. This way we are able to use the authorized version for each name via the metadata entry screen. While initially time-consuming, the effort of creating new name authority records after the original loading of names has been minimal, with the addition of only a few dozen new names each month.

Discussion

Overall, the implementation of name authority in our collections has been successful. Although we do not plan to attempt system-wide control of all names in our collections, we now have the ability to establish authority records that we deem important for any project. For example, the Texas Fashion Collection[17] has a large number of names that are frequently entered in metadata. Using authority records for the names in this collection would make metadata entry more streamlined and allow for contextual linking, since some of the designers may have established authorities in other systems. Additionally, we have started using the Name App to better define current and historic names for buildings on the UNT campus, which is useful for some of the local archival collections we are digitizing that document UNT's history.

We have found that incorporating name authority control into existing digital library collections can be accomplished in a straightforward and sustainable way. The ability to integrate authorized names during the metadata entry process has helped to streamline this process and is directly related to basing our authority work on a framework that supports a connection between authorities and metadata records. One outcome of this work that we did not expect was the interest from many other institutions around the country in doing this same sort of work with their local names; once they heard about our UNT Name App, several of them wanted to install the tool for their local institutions. Initially, we were not ready to make the code publicly available, but in early 2015 we released the source code under an Open Source Licence on the UNT Libraries' Github site under the project name 'django-name.'[18] Hopefully, by making this code available, we will enable others to repeat, modify and improve upon the process that we used.

Future steps

There is a continuing need in libraries and other cultural heritage organizations – such as archives and museums – to engage in name authority activities. Although the wide range of existing name authority projects demonstrates recognition of this need and the connection to functionality for end-users, the diversity in this area also shows the need for concerted efforts on multiple fronts to make headway on such a huge task. Even with various national and international efforts, there is still a need for local institutions to manage and curate names that are important to the lifecycle of information resources in our academic institutions. However, to ensure that these efforts will have the largest impact and be compatible with other projects, we should do our best to make sure that contributions to name authority work meet standards and expectations within the wider community, so that users at other institutions or outside the library sphere can take advantage of the work. By starting with the five stars of open linked data and then using an iterative approach, such as the one described in this chapter, we can capitalize on local efforts to create a co-operative compilation that can be shared openly and continue to grow well into the future.

References

Berners-Lee, T. (2006) *Linked Data*, 7 July,
    www.w3.org/DesignIssues/LinkedData.html.
Ilik, V. (2014) Cataloger Makeover: creating Non-MARC Name Authorities,
    Cataloging & Classification Quarterly, **53** (3–4), 382–98.
OCLC (2012a) VIAFbot *Edits 250,000 Wikipedia Articles to Reciprocate All Links from VIAF into Wikipedia*, 7 December, www.oclc.org/research/news/2012/12-07a.html.
OCLC (2012b), *OCLC Adds Linked Data to WorldCat.org*, 20 June,
    www.oclc.org/news/releases/2012/201238.en.html.
OCLC (2015) *VIAF: Virtual International Authority File*, www.oclc.org/viaf.en.html.
Salo, D. (2009) Name Authority Control in Institutional Repositories, *Cataloging & Classification Quarterly*, **47** (3–4), 249–61.
Tarver, H., Waugh, L., Phillips, M. and Hicks, W. (2013) *Implementing Name Authority Control into Institutional Repositories: a staged approach*,
    http://digital.library.unt.edu/ark:/67531/metadc172365.
Texas A&M University Libraries (2015) *ORCID and Other Researcher Identifiers*,
    14 April, http://guides.library.tamu.edu/content.php?pid=553864&sid=4564757.
Tillett, B. B. (1989) Considerations for Authority Control in the Online Environment,
    Cataloging & Classification Quarterly, **9** (3), 1–11.
University of North Texas Libraries (2015) *Input Guidelines for Descriptive Metadata*,
    www.library.unt.edu/digital-projects-unit/input-guidelines-descriptive-metadata.

Websites

1   Library of Congress Name Authority File, http://id.loc.gov/authorities/names.html.

2 Virtual International Authority File (VIAF), https://viaf.org.

3 Open Researcher and Contributor ID (ORCID), http://orcid.org.

4 International Standard Name Identifier (ISNI), www.isni.org.

5 The Portal to Texas History, http://texashistory.unt.edu.

6 UNT Digital Library, http://digital.library.unt.edu.

7 The Gateway to Oklahoma History, http://gateway.okhistory.org.

8 UNT Vocabularies, http://digital2.library.unt.edu/vocabularies.

9 UNT Name App, http://digital2.library.unt.edu/name.

10 Metadata Authority Description Schema (MADS), www.loc.gov/standards/mads.

11 Schema.org, http://schema.org.

12 Google Scholar Citations, https://scholar.google.com/intl/en-US/scholar/citations.html.

13 Amazon, www.amazon.com.

14 WorldCat Identities, www.worldcat.org/identities.

15 Open Library: Authors, https://openlibrary.org/authors.

16 UNT Open Access Policy, http://openaccess.unt.edu/unt-open-access-policy.

17 Texas Fashion Collection, http://digital.library.unt.edu/explore/collections/TXFC.

18 UNT Name App source code, https://github.com/unt-libraries/django-name.

Index